THE
STREET LAW
HANDBOOK

THE
STREET LAW
HANDBOOK

Surviving Sex, Drugs, and Petty Crime

by
Neeraja Viswanathan, Esq.

BLOOMSBURY

Published by Bloomsbury, New York and London
Distributed to the trade by Holtzbrinck Publishers

All papers used by Bloomsbury are natural, recyclable products made
from wood grown in well-managed forests. The manufacturing
processes conform to the environmental
regulations of the country of origin.

Library of Congress Cataloging-in-Publication Data

Viswanathan, Neeraja.
The street law handbook : surviving sex, drugs, and petty crime /
Neeraja Viswanathan.
p. cm.
ISBN 1-58234-491-4 (hardback)
1. Criminal law—United States—Popular works.
2. Criminal procedure—United States—Popular works. I. Title.

KF9219.6.V57 2004
345.73—dc22
2004006341

First U.S. Edition 2004

1 3 5 7 9 10 8 6 4 2

Typeset by Palimpsest Book Production Limited,
Polmont, Stirlingshire, Scotland
Printed in the United States of America
by Quebecor World Fairfield

To
my friends
and
my family
(and to all those people for whom the terms
are interchangeable)

and
to Jupi

CONTENTS

Introduction

When you become a lawyer, you become fair game for everybody with a legal problem. From their noisy, naked neighbor to their lawsuit against Grandma's estate, everybody's got some legal issue that they know you're just dying to advise them on. Usually at a cocktail party or in the middle of the ninth inning of the World Series.

The thing is, they all have the same kind of questions. Will I get in trouble for my little marijuana plant? Can I get away with having sex in the backseat of my car? Do I have to answer a cop's questions? Unless you're hanging around with legal scholars or hardened criminals, no one's really interested in the Rule against Perpetuities or federal sentencing guidelines. Who else but lawyers would care about those things? People want practical answers to simple questions that affect their day-to-day life.

And so *The Street Law Handbook* is born.

Listen, if you've got a joint in your pocket, you're breaking the law. But do you know which law? If you're going to walk out of your house with that joint, don't you want to know what your rights are? (And yes, you do have rights. Even murderers have rights.)

Without knowing it, you could be committing a crime right now. You could be playing your stereo too loud or jaywalking or drinking from an open container. Most of the time, you won't get into serious trouble; you'll get a bored patrolman who will write you a citation. But in this post 9-11 climate, virtually any infraction can become a big problem. Think about this: the Supreme Court recently ruled that cops can arrest people and bring them in even for minor traffic offenses. That means if you run a red light or don't have your seat belt on, a cop could theoretically handcuff you, arrest you, impound your car, and haul you off to jail. So to really know your rights, you need to know some simple facts about the law. Here are the basics:

There are two types of cases: civil and criminal.

Street Law Concept #1: Civil Versus Criminal Cases
Civil cases usually occur between private citizens. Criminal cases—also known as prosecutions—are "offenses against society," and usually between a private citizen and law enforcement.

The government represents "society" and prosecutes you for your crimes. The government can be local, state, or federal. An example of a civil lawsuit is when your neighbor hits your car with his. In that case, you're suing him for the damages. A criminal action is where your neighbor shoots at you. In that case, even if he doesn't hit you, it's an act against society, and the government prosecutes him. This book does not cover civil lawsuits.

The government is represented by a prosecutor; you are usually represented by a defense attorney or a public defender.

> **Street Law Concept #2: Prosecutor**
> A prosecutor is the attorney who represents the government. A prosecutor can be federal (known as a federal prosecutor or a U.S. attorney) or state (known as a state prosecutor or a district attorney).

> **Street Law Concept #3: Defense Attorneys Versus Public Defenders**
> A defense attorney is an attorney who has his own private practice. You pay for him as you would any other attorney. A public defender is provided to you by the court. He is either an employee of a governmental defense organization (such as Legal Aid) or a private attorney who takes cases at reduced fees.

The prosecutor's job is to prove you guilty beyond a reasonable doubt by using witnesses or other evidence to prove his case. In court, you will be known as the *defendant,* and until the prosecution proves its case, you're "not guilty" (and you can say things like "I *allegedly* ran naked through the street').

In all states, crimes are usually split up into three categories:

CATEGORY	DEFINITION
Felony	An offense that is punishable by at least one year in prison, and/or a fine. Think murder, rape, being a don in the mob
Misdemeanor	An offense that will get you less than one year in prison, and/or a fine. Think trespassing, disorderly

CATEGORY	DEFINITION
	conduct, running naked through the street
Violation/Citation/Petty Offense	An offense that is so minor you'll usually just have to pay a fine. Think noise violations, jaywalking, not having your dog on a leash

Felonies and misdemeanors can be broken up into different "**classes**" or "**degrees**." For example, a Class A misdemeanor can carry a maximum penalty of one year, a Class B misdemeanor could carry a maximum penalty of six months, and so on. Similarly, when you are found guilty of second-degree murder, you might get twenty-five years to life, while first-degree murder (murder of a cop, for example) could get you the death penalty.

Okay, so maybe you've watched a couple of episodes of *Law & Order* and you know all this. But do you remember the trial, with those twelve friendly jurors listening to your side of the story? Forget about it. Frankly, trials are expensive and can take forever. In most criminal cases, a defendant will reach some sort of agreement with the prosecution (a *plea bargain*) in exchange for a lighter sentence.

The Street Law Handbook is designed to be easy to read. *Penalty charts* show you the maximum state fines and jail sentences you can get for certain offenses. There might also be violations of federal laws or city ordinances in addition to the listed penalties, but this book doesn't cover them. Not all crimes carry federal penalties, and city or local laws don't usually have heavy repercussions.

Furthermore, the charts provide the penalty for your first offense—it'll be more than what's listed for your second or third time around and, in many cases, upgraded to a felony. The charts also apply to straightforward cases without aggravating circumstances (e.g., you're not selling drugs near a school or masturbating in front of a minor). Finally, all crimes listed can include a fine or jail time or both.

Make sure to read the wild and wacky cases that illustrate the law and show you how nuts people can be. And the *street law concepts* will give you handy, bite-size definitions of legal issues that might apply to you.

So . . . let the fun begin!

Disclaimer

Before diving into the fascinating world of street law, here are some important words of caution. While this book contains general references to certain laws in effect at the time of the writing of this book, it was not written as a legal guide or as a substitute for legal advice from qualified attorneys. The wisdom you will find in these pages is, don't commit crimes, and don't break any laws. If you ignore this advice, then you are proceeding at your own risk.

So why do you need *The Street Law Handbook*?

Well, in the real world, people like to see what they can get away with. And no matter what your mother or your boss or the president says, even good people break the law occasionally—even if they know better.

Here's what this book is not:

It is *not* a how-to guide on being a criminal. (And please understand, if you break a big law or a small law and are found guilty, you fit the category of criminal. Period.)

Despite its title, this is not a complete handbook of the law. The law is fluid—it changes regularly. It's also different from state to state, even city to city. Furthermore, there is no way to know exactly how the law is going to be interpreted. That can vary from judge to judge, day to day. These are just general guidelines. Rely on them at your own risk.

This book is *not* a substitute for the advice of a good attorney. Waving this book at your trial is not going to impress the judge or the jury. Quoting it to your arresting officer will probably make your life a lot worse.

It is *not* intended to be read for anything more than entertainment purposes. Again, if you're tempted to break the law, skip ahead to chapter 5, "Worst-Case Scenario: Go Directly to Jail." If that doesn't dissuade you, watch an episode of *Cops*. Or *Oz*.

This book is *not* a substitute for common sense. If you're in a situation and you think the advice in *The Street Law Handbook* goes against common sense, then trust your instincts. Don't treat this book like a crystal ball that will predict your legal future. If your gut is giving you better advice than what's written here, then go with your gut.

In plain, simple legalese, the publishers and the author and all those associated with the creation of this book expressly disclaim any liability, arrest, or injury that may arise from any use (improper or proper) of the information in this book. All the information contained in this book is taken directly from case law, published reports, and legal treatises, but the author does not guarantee the accuracy of the information.

That said, enjoy!

A NOTE ON SOURCES

The information contained in *The Street Law Handbook* comes from a variety of sources—namely:

- Law school (kids—don't try this one at home!)
- Interviews with police officers, district attorneys and prosecutors, public defenders, defense attorneys, doctors and legal scholars from various states and jurisdictions
- Interviews with individuals who, for various reasons, have experience with breaking the law, and on occasion, getting away with it. Particularly on the subject of controlled substances
- Newspapers, news journals, and reports published via the Internet
- Public records and statutes
- Court documents, mostly found on a legal database called Westlaw.com
- Legal textbooks and dictionaries

A word about the cases: they're all real, found in court documents or newspaper reports. The details are all accurate; only the names have been changed to protect the foolish and not-so-innocent. Virtually all of the information found in this book—including the cases—is available to the public, and if you are a particularly determined sort you can find out further details and explanations for yourself. (You might need to pay a fee on Westlaw.com.) The Internet is a particularly good source of information on most subjects found in the *Handbook*.

Chapter 1

Get Your Buzz On: Weed, Coke, Crack, Acid . . . and What You Need to Know About the War on Drugs

INTRODUCTION

Whatever the government tells you about the War on Drugs, one thing is true: Americans love to get high. And it seems that the more the government tries to crack down on the users and the dealers, the more the drug trade flourishes.

Are drugs bad for you? Depends on your definition of "bad." Few people would argue that the harder stuff (crack, cocaine, heroin) isn't addictive. There's no doubt that extended marijuana use can kill brain cells and lower your sperm count. And as for what you might be cooking up at home—ecstasy, crystal meth, to name a few—well, who knows what that stuff might do to you in the long term?

But guess what? Knowing that doesn't stop many people from dabbling. And *The Street Law Handbook* does not judge. If you want to try your hand at occasional narcotic use, then that's your decision. But you might just want to keep reading, to see what you're getting yourself into—and what it will take to keep your sweet self out of trouble.

First Things First: Federal Drug Schedules

What makes a drug a drug? Or, specifically, what makes a drug illegal?

Street Law Concept #4: Controlled Substances

The government is worried about these drugs because they have a high potential for abuse or addiction. Therefore, these drugs are strictly regulated or even outlawed. Common controlled substances include narcotics (morphine, heroin), stimulants (cocaine), depressants (Valium), hallucinogens (LSD, peyote), and weed.

Now, yes, that can be a no-brainer. Even the most goody-two-shoes schoolboy knows *some* of the baddies: marijuana, cocaine, heroin. But what about mescaline? Ketamine? Fentanyl? What does GHB stand for? ("Gamma hydroxybutyrate," in case you were *really* interested.) Sound confusing? Welcome to the wonderful world of drug scheduling.

THE LONG ARM OF THE LAW: Armed raids on head shops? The DEA rerouting visitors of paraphernalia Web sites? Denying federal aid to students with even one previous marijuana possession? If there are guidelines on the War on Drugs, no one seems too interested in them. Back in 1991, the Supreme Court held that possession of approximately a kilo of coke could legally result in life *without parole*. Ten years later, with Ashcroft in charge, it's just getting scarier.

The federal government classifies certain controlled substances in a system of schedules, labeled from Schedule

I (most controlled) to Schedule V (least controlled). Many states follow the federal government's general reasoning, if not method (though there are exceptions: for example, New York has an entirely separate—and more lenient—section for marijuana). Here's a quick summary:

Schedule I: The Big No-No's. According to the Feds, these drugs have no recognized medical value and shouldn't be used even under medical supervision. They are also likely to cause dependency or be abused, so even doctors can't write a prescription for them.

Common Schedule I Drugs

- LSD (acid): a hallucinogenic, may result in visions of pink elephants
- Heroin: also known as smack, the choice of Trainspotters everywhere
- MDMA: the main ingredient in ecstasy
- Peyote: cactus containing mescaline; call it narcotics Southwest-style
- Mushrooms: not shiitake, just those containing psilocybin or other hallucinogens
- Marijuana: even medicinal marijuana is illegal under federal law
- GHB: a favorite of ravers and the techno crowd

Schedule II: Bad Stuff with Redeeming Qualities. Schedule II drugs don't appear much different from Schedule I drugs. These drugs are considered easy to abuse and result in physical dependency. However, they have some medical uses and may be prescribed in rare or unique instances. The process to do so, however, is lengthy and restrictive.

Common Schedule II Drugs

- Cocaine: an eighties Brat Pack favorite
- Crack: cocaine's dirty downtown cousin
- Phencyclidine: they call it angel dust or PCP on the street
- Opium: kinda uncommon—but maybe there's a den in your neighborhood
- Ritalin and Seconal: don't let them bring you down
- Codeine: not the stuff in your cough syrup—this means morphine

Schedule III: For Doctor's Use Only. The United States recognizes that these drugs have medical value; therefore, they may be prescribed. (And not just to humans: ketamine, for example, is an animal tranquilizer.) These drugs can be abused and can make their users physically or psychologically dependent; however, they're still not as bad as Schedule I or II drugs.

Common Schedule III Drugs

- Ketamine: also known as Special K
- Secobarbital: an ingredient in a lot of prescriptions designed to mellow you out
- Anabolic steroids: breakfast of bodybuilders

Schedule IV: Probably in Your Medicine Cabinet Already. These drugs have less potential for abuse, and the dependency—according to the Feds, anyway—is far less than those in Schedules I–III. These drugs can be prescribed for medical treatment— usually for bored socialites or stressed-out supermodels.

Common Schedule IV Drugs

- Valium: the 1970s housewife favorite

- Xanax: when Prince Valium can't make it
- Rohypnol: designed to mellow you out . . . but used by date rapists everywhere

Schedule V: Everything Else. These controlled substances are often widely used for medical treatment. The abuse and dependency potential is less than for those drugs in Schedule IV. Example: your cough syrup.

So that's the Feds. The odds are good, however, that you will not be busted by the Feds. As a recreational user, you're probably small fry to Uncle Sam . . . until you deliver six bricks of cocaine every Sunday to your local drug cartel. So, while you should never be smug or careless (you could meet a bored DEA agent with nothing better to do), the odds are that the narcotics laws that you'll really need to worry about will be state, not federal.

Below is a list of commonly used and controlled substances, complete with penalty charts in various cities. Before you continue, however, here's a quick editorial note: *possession of ANY amount of a controlled substance can get you busted for possession.* The law isn't clear on how picky the cops can be, but some cases out there discuss how many seeds of dried marijuana constitute possession, and how many grams of coke result in a felony. They can be that particular. That said, most states have quantity measures to prevent an indiscretion (and misdemeanor) from being a felony. But in some cases, the narcotics (particularly cocaine, crack, and heroin) are such baddies that you'll be in felony territory before you know it. So keep reading, pay attention, and start learning the metric system. (Yes, it comes in handy, just as your grade-school teacher promised.)

> **California Dreaming**
>
> California is by far the best state to possess drugs in. Under the penal code, virtually every first-time possession case is treated to something called diversion. This is the state-authorized program that's similar to probation. Essentially, you'll sign up for a treatment program, report to a probation officer, and upon completion of the whole program, it'll be as if your arrest never happened. Usually diversion takes anywhere from eighteen months to three years. In California, for nonviolent first-time drug offenders, diversion is *mandatory*, regardless of what drug you possess. Second-time drug possession will get you up to approximately two years and/or a $1,000 fine. And the minute you're charged for sale, it's a whole different ball game of serious jail time.

WEIGHTS AND MEASURES
Marijuana

Marijuana is one of the oldest narcotics around, dating as far back as 4000 B.C. in China. The plant was often used as medicine in parts of India, South America, Africa, and the Middle East. It might be tolerated in enlightened countries such as the Netherlands, but in this country, a weed smoker is arrested every forty-five seconds. Possession of the Good Herb is illegal in all fifty states, and you can be subject to prosecution by both state and federal governments. Despite all this, pot is the most popular narcotic in America, and chances are, if you don't smoke yourself, you know someone who does.

THOSE DISCO YEARS: Despite the leisure suits, the 1970s weren't all bad. The Controlled Substance Act of 1970 removed required minimum prison sentences for marijuana possession and reduced penalties for marijuana in general. This was a marked change from earlier decades, which treated marijuana no differently from heroin or cocaine. And despite the Nixon administration's frantic war against drugs, marijuana activists began to advocate decriminalization in the 1970s. In 1977, President Jimmy Carter argued that marijuana should be decriminalized. In fact, the Senate judiciary committee voted in October 1977 to decriminalize marijuana, but reversed its decision when faced with powerful Republican opposition. The end result? In the seventies, the federal government spent $85 billion on the war against marijuana alone—about $75 billion more than in the 1960s. (It only got worse: the Feds spent $200 billion against weed in the 1980s. Money well spent? You be the judge.)

Facts

Appearance: Cannabis leaves usually have five points and must be prepared. The marijuana that's fit to smoke is a green/gray/brown mixture of dried and prepared leaves, stems, seeds, and flowers.

Accessories: Bongs made out of anything (water bottles, apples, etc.) or professionally made glass or plastic ones. Small ceramic, wood, or metal pipes. Rolling papers, screens, and roach clips (to hold your joint). Snackable treats. Groovy music. Deep thoughts.

Dosage: Usually sold in eighths of one ounce. One ounce is 28.5 grams, so an eighth is about 3.5 grams. Since this is a measure of weight, appearance may vary. Generally, try the Rule of Thumb: an eighth of decent weed is the size of a man's thumb from tip to palm

and should get anywhere from fifteen to twenty-five
people high. Alternatively, half a teaspoon will provide
four to eight hits. Usually one to three hits should get
you high. It may also be sold in dime bags, which is
$10 of weed.

Chemical makeup: Delta-9-tetrahydrocannabinol (THC),
located in the resins of flowers from female plants.
THC—which is similar to the compounds found in
hashish—is one of nearly a hundred or so chemical
compounds found in marijuana. Some of these chemicals are just plain carcinogens, like those in cigarettes
(in fact, one joint can result in the same amount of
smoke as four tobacco cigarettes). However, there are
also hundreds of chemicals—many carcinogens—in
coffee.

Method of ingestion: Weed is usually smoked in handmade
joints, or in bongs. However, it can be distilled or
baked in a wide variety of recipes, brownies in particular. The high from oral ingestion is very different,
starting slower and lasting longer.

Buzz begins: You'll start feeling high in about ten minutes.

Type of buzz: Mellow. Weed can result in feelings of extreme
relaxation and peace of mind, relief from physical pain.

Buzz duration: One to three hours, peaking about twenty to
thirty minutes after ingestion. Mellow and spacey feelings can last for a long time afterward, depending on
how much you did.

Negative effects: According to the DEA, prolonged use can
result in possible respiratory infections, short- and long-
term memory loss, impaired motor skills and reflexes,
decreased attention span, and lethargy. Weed makes
some people antsy and paranoid, even in small doses.

Almost everyone develops munchies—you'll start getting hungry as the high wears off.

Tolerance: Up to 10 percent of users get addicted. You may become tolerant if you do high doses often; however, it will go away if you stop for a while. Withdrawal symptoms are minor.

Penalties for Possession The good news for all you potheads out there is that, in most cases (and in most states) you probably won't get anywhere near the maximum if all you did was quietly carry a little weed. In fact, a cop might even look the other way or let you off with a warning. Please understand that this is not the official law of the land; it just happens sometimes. Obviously, it depends on where you are, but because of legalization efforts and marijuana's rumored medicinal properties, weed is the drug least likely to get you in big trouble. Ultimately, it's like jaywalking . . . you may think a cop is nuts to arrest you for something so petty, but he still has the legal right to do it.

Chart 1: Marijuana Penalties

City	Maximum Fine	Maximum Jail Time	Details
Los Angeles (28.5 grams/ 1 ounce)	$100	None	First possession of an ounce or less of marijuana is not an arrestable offense. Increased penalty for possession on school grounds. License suspension for

City	Maximum Fine	Maximum Jail Time	Details
			convicted offenders under 21
District of Columbia (amount not specified)	$1,000	Up to 6 months	First offenders are eligible for probation, with charges dismissed upon completion
Miami (20 grams or less)	$1,000	1 year	Any amount over 20 grams results in a felony conviction
Chicago (up to 30 grams)	$2,500	1 year	The penalties are more lenient for amounts less than 10 or 2.5 grams. First-time offenders are eligible for 24-month probation for amounts less than 30 grams, and the charges will be dismissed at the end
Las Vegas (any amount, first offense)	$600	None	Automatic probation and possible drug treatment for first and second offense (fine for second is $1,000). Third offense can lead to 1 year and/or $2,500

City	Maximum Fine	Maximum Jail Time	Details
			fine. Possession of less than 1 ounce by persons under 21 years of age is a felony (1–4 years, $5,000)
New York (less than 25 grams, first offense)	$100	None/ probation	Second offense: $200, no time. Subsequent offense: $250, up to 15 days. Possession of 25 grams to 2 ounces results in up to $500, up to 3 months
Dallas (less than 2 ounces, or 57 grams)	$2,000	Up to 6 months	After 4 ounces, possession results in minimum 180 days incarceration and $10,000 fine

Ecstasy

Known as X, XTC, E, or Adam, ecstasy promises just what it says—a feeling of such love and happiness that strangers become your friends. Commonplace all over the world at huge clubs and raves, ecstasy pills are popped like the mints they resemble. Ecstasy is chemically known as methylenedioxymethamphetamine, or MDMA. No one really calls it that, though. And unlike marijuana, ecstasy is a man-made chemical. First patented in Germany in 1913, MDMA was created for possible medical use. It didn't really show up on the medical radars until 1953, when it was tested by none other than the U.S. military. Over the next few decades, scientists and doctors studied it for possible therapeutic use. MDMA didn't really hit the streets as a "fun drug" until the mid-eighties, which resulted in a prompt federal ban on any use or research.

Facts

Appearance: Small tablets, usually white or pink and resembling certain mints sold in a popular chain of coffee-houses. Usually embossed with a logo—Mitsubishi, for example. Ecstasy can also come in powder form, but this is rare.

Accessories: Pacifier (you'll grind your teeth), glowsticks, dust masks with Vicks VapoRub (the smell will supposedly get you higher), water bottle (filled with water; you'll need it).

Dosage: One pill to start—usually no more than two will be required. Pills vary in size, but you can usually fit two pills on a penny.

Chemical makeup: Each pill should average 80 to 125 milligrams of MDMA. There will be other ingredients—ketamine, LSD, aspirin, caffeine.

Method of ingestion: Eat it. You can snort the powder. Injecting is possible, but rare and fraught with major health issues.

Buzz begins: You'll start rolling in twenty to forty-five minutes.

Type of buzz: Groovy. Strangers become your friends and friends become family. Spontaneous understanding of techno music. You'll want to touch things, and you'll love everyone around you. (See later sections regarding sex in public if you are tempted to literally do just that.) Wired and wakeful.

Buzz duration: The high will last three to four hours. For

another one to seven hours you'll be hyper and sleepless and probably still happy.

Negative effects: Suppressed appetite, severe dehydration, panic attacks, involuntary muscle movement, loss of memory, rapid heartbeat, possible heatstroke or permanent damage to brain. Dehydration is a real problem—drink lots of water while rolling. Also, the Day After (not always the day after, sometimes a couple days after), your brain is lacking serotonin (happy juice), and you will not just feel hungover—you'll actually be depressed. This can last for up to five days.

Tolerance: Ecstasy can work for you twenty times, and the twenty-first, you might have become immune to its effects. It's hard to predict.

Penalties for Possession Though many people swear ecstasy has therapeutic use, MDMA is a Schedule I substance. That means the penalties for possession are usually pretty harsh. Lately, the government has been cracking down hard on ecstasy and other club drugs.

Chart 2: Ecstasy Penalties

City	Maximum Fine	Maximum Jail Time
Los Angeles	Diversion	Diversion
District of Columbia (amount not specified)	$1,000	6 months
Miami (less than 10 grams)	$5,000	Up to 5 years
Chicago (less than 15 grams)	$25,000	1–3 years

City	Maximum Fine	Maximum Jail Time
Las Vegas (up to 4 grams)	$5,000	1–4 years
New York (any amount)	$1,000	1 year
Dallas (less than 1 gram)	$10,000	180 days to 2 years

Mushrooms

Psychoactive mushrooms were favorites among hippies and those looking for a "naturally" psychedelic good time. The high originates from the psilocybin found in these mushrooms, and the high is supposed to be like a low-level LSD trip. "Magic" mushrooms have been used for centuries by many Native American and Central American cultures for a "spiritual" or "alternative reality" experience. Psilocybin was made illegal in the United States in 1968, thereby ending the spiritual trip for many. Approximately 180 types of psychoactive mushrooms are known, usually originating from the genera *Psilocybe, Panaeolus,* or *Copelandia.*

Facts

Appearance: Like gray or tan mushrooms. *Wet* means they resemble your pizza toppings. *Dried* is dehydrated mushrooms. Mostly indistinguishable from edible or poisonous mushrooms, except some types bruise blue when handled.

Accessories: Nature, citrus fruits, Jell-O, crayons, glowsticks (lights are nice). Nature is the big one—if you have access to the outdoors, use it. Sometimes materials for a religious journey. Aquarium and brown rice sugar (among other items) if you are growing them.

Dosage: One to five grams wet, ten to forty grams dried— alternatively, one to two big mushrooms or four to eighteen small mushrooms. Will vary in appearance as each mushroom is different.

Chemical makeup: Each mushroom has less than 2 percent psilocybin. It's powerful stuff.

Method of ingestion: Eat it. Because they don't taste very good, they can be used in recipes. Sweeten with honey, mix with orange juice, steep in tea, or grind into powder. Generally, the stomach should be a little empty.

Buzz begins: Ten to twenty-five minutes after ingestion.

Type of buzz: Trippy. Not dissimilar to small doses of LSD. Heightened awareness leads to a shift in senses. More energy. Deep contemplation of ordinary objects. Possible hallucinations. Your perception of the physical world changes.

Buzz duration: Four to six hours. Afterward, you'll probably still feel wired for a while.

Negative effects: Nausea, dizziness, and cramps. Do not do mushrooms in unfamiliar surroundings or when upset, as they will only heighten the experience. A bad trip is always possible and can make you paranoid, fearful, or panicky. Possible flashbacks.

Tolerance: Not addictive. However, if you do it once a week for a month or so, your high will probably become weak and pitiful.

Penalties for Possession 'Shrooms are a federal Schedule I substance. However, states vary wildly in their treatment of magic mushroom possession. In Colorado, for example, possession is a Class 3 felony, punishable by a $2,000 fine. In Florida, possession of 'shrooms is legal. In Delaware, possession is a misdemeanor, but first-time offenders are eligible for probation.

Most states don't prohibit 'shrooms specifically; they simply prohibit any "container" of the substances of psilocybin or psilocin, including 'shrooms. However, it's legal to possess the spores of magic mushrooms in all states except California and Oregon. This is because the spores don't contain the ingredient psilocybin, while the mature mushroom does. Generally, the courts must show that you were aware of the psychoactive properties of the mushrooms you were growing/picking. If you genuinely thought they were ordinary mushrooms for your pasta sauce, the government will find it hard to prove its case.

Chart 3: Magic Mushroom Penalties

City	Maximum Fine	Maximum Jail Time
Los Angeles (any amount)	Diversion	Diversion
District of Columbia (amount not specified)	$1,000	1 year
Miami (less than 10 grams)	N/A	N/A
Chicago (any amount)	$15,000	1–3 years. Possible probation for first-time offenses
Las Vegas (less than 4 grams)	$5,000	1–4 years. Possible probation for first-time offenses

City	Maximum Fine	Maximum Jail Time
New York (up to 25 milligrams)	$1,000	1 year
Dallas (less than 1 gram)	$10,000	180 days to 2 years

Methamphetamines

Meth, also known as crystal meth, or speed, is making a comeback. Since it's easy to manufacture, homegrown meth labs are being set up (and busted) all over, giving it a reputation as a "trailer park" high. Purists claim that speed will kill the happy vibe of a good rave. Others swear by the energy rush. When you think of the drug that keeps truckers driving all day and all night, or bikers trekking across the country, you're thinking of speed. Methamphetamines are a type of amphetamine that contain the chemical methyl (hence the name). Amphetamines have been around (and prescribed) since the late nineteenth century, but meth was discovered in Japan in the 1920s. Amphetamines were often given to soldiers during World War II, and the usage of meth in particular skyrocketed as an injected version came on the market. Meth use was only curtailed in the 1970 Controlled Substance Act. It is still manufactured legally in the United States under the name Desoxyn and is used to treat certain cases of ADD.

Facts

Appearance: Odorless, white substance with a bitter taste. Occasionally gray, pink, or brown, due to impurities. In crystal form, known as ice. Water can form on these crystals. In tablet form, four pills fit onto a penny.

Accessories: Someone to talk to, dance music, or a really messy apartment to clean. Water.

Dosage: One gram of meth should be three to four hits. This depends on its strength and other ingredients. Overdose is possible at amounts as low as fifty milligrams.

Chemical makeup: Most speed bought on the street is only 2 to 5 percent meth. Many, many other ingredients may be in it; talcum powder, cocaine, baking soda, Epsom salts, heroin, you name it. There's no way to tell.

Method of ingestion: Various. Tablets are eaten, powder may be snorted or smoked. Ice is smoked in an ice pipe or on foil over a low flame. Can be injected.

Buzz begins: You will start tweaking almost immediately if you snort or inject. It can take up to an hour if you eat it.

Type of buzz: Hyperactive. Possible feelings of invulnerability or sexual arousal. Sleeplessness.

Buzz duration: Four to six hours. You probably won't be yourself for another ten to fifteen hours.

Negative effects: Twitchiness, hyperventilation, slow reflexes, and itching welts on the skin. Severe weight loss and lack of appetite. In more severe cases, meth causes paranoia, depression, extreme moodiness, and extreme aggressiveness. Possible insomnia. Bad adulterants can kill you. Extended meth use (or one just really bad hit) can cause permanent psychological problems, brain damage, or even death.

Tolerance: Pretty addictive. The comedown is bad and similar to the Day After experience of ecstasy.

Penalties for Possession In the current climate, meth possession is dangerous—it's the federal and state authorities' drug bust of choice. Meth possession, however, is infinitely preferable to meth manufacturing, which causes huge problems not only with law enforcement, but also with your neighbors, your air quality, and the health of anyone within a radius of a few yards.

Chart 4: Methamphetamine Penalties

City	Maximum Fine	Maximum Jail Time
Los Angeles (any amount)	Diversion	Diversion
District of Columbia (amount not specified)	$1,000	Up to 1 year
Miami (up to 14 grams)	$5,000	Up to 5 years
Chicago (up to 15 grams)	$25,000	1–3 years
Las Vegas (up to 4 grams)	$5,000	1–4 years
New York (up to 0.5 ounces/14 grams)	$1,000	Up to 1 year
Dallas (up to 1 gram)	$10,000	180 days to 2 years

LSD (Acid)
Timothy Leary loved it. Aldous Huxley wrote on it. Even Cary Grant supposedly did it. In the sixties, it seemed that everyone was tripping on little white tabs. More than a

drug, acid was touted as a whole new experience—changing your reality, your personality, and your brain cells. LSD (lysergic acid diethylamide) was discovered in the 1920s by Dr. Albert Hoffman, who didn't actually experience its hallucinatory effects until the 1940s. Technically, LSD is synthetic, though it has some natural or organic elements. After a host of experiments by various governments, LSD was deemed a danger to society just as the hippies got ahold of it. In the sixties and seventies people were tuning in and dropping out—and occasionally seeing some really trippy things. As a psychoactive drug, acid is incredibly powerful. While coke is measured in milligrams, LSD is measured in micrograms. Since one microgram is 0.000001 gram, you can tell that this is potent stuff.

Facts

Appearance: White, odorless powder. Usually in small tablets, little gelatin cubes, sugar cubes, or on "blotters"—sheets of papers with designs that have little dots. Each dot is a hit. Liquid can be dropped onto candies.

Accessories: Lights, especially moving lights. Trippy music. Good friends and comfortable surroundings.

Dosage: Twenty-five to 150 micrograms. Twenty-five micrograms is about a few grains of salt. In the sixties the average dose was two hundred to four hundred micrograms.

Chemical makeup: Few adulterants, given the tiny dose.

Method of ingestion: Eat it. Or lick the blotter dot.

Buzz begins: From thirty to ninety minutes after ingestion. Peaks within hours.

Type of buzz: Hypnotic. At first, colors look sharper and senses are heightened. Then moving objects leave trails.

Lights become fascinating. Dreamy and hallucinatory. The peaks are rumored to be a mystical or transcendent experience.

Buzz duration: Four to six hours. You'll feel high for three to five hours more, and you probably won't be able to sleep for up to ten hours after ingestion.

Negative Effects: Terrifying bad trips. You may become paranoid, aggressive, scared. In such cases, reduce stimulation and be around friends. No TV. Stay calm and be in familiar surroundings. If you are not in a good mental state before doing LSD, you are asking for trouble. Other effects: impaired depth and space perception, rapid heart rate, sweats, and goose bumps. Don't try to rely on your senses. Fear of a loss of control, of insanity or death. Serious depression after the high wears off. Flashbacks possible weeks or months later.

Tolerance: It is easy to develop a tolerance to acid, and you'll need more to recapture your high. However, LSD is not that addictive.

Penalties for Possession Prosecutors aren't impressed with LSD's grooviness. Because it's a Schedule I drug, you can face harsh penalties for possession. However, since LSD is measured in micrograms, it's kind of hard to be conspicuous about acid possession. A dot dropped on a mint or SweeTARTS or piece of gum is virtually impossible to detect unless the cop has his eye on you for some other reason anyway. LSD blotters are often colorfully decorated, and the ubiquitous LSD happy face is a dead giveaway. Without these, cops can find it hard to identify LSD users.

Chart 5: LSD Penalties

City	Maximum Fine	Maximum Jail Time
Los Angeles (any amount)	Diversion	Diversion
District of Columbia (amount not specified)	$1,000	6 months
Miami (up to 1 gram)	$5,000	Up to 5 years
Chicago (up to 15 grams)	$25,000	1–3 years
Las Vegas (up to 4 grams)	$5,000	1–4 years
New York (less than 1 milligram)	$1,000	1 year
Dallas (up to 20 abuse units)	$10,000	180 days to 2 years

Cocaine and Crack

A mirror on a table, neat lines of white powder, rolled-up hundred-dollar bills . . . nothing said the 1980s like cocaine. However, cocaine (also known as blow, snow, nose candy, lines) has been around since 3000 B.C. Derived from coco leaves (not to be confused with cacao leaves, which make chocolate), cocaine was a stimulant initially thought to have powerful medicinal qualities. Freud even recommended cocaine to treat morphine addiction. While the pharmaceutical companies grew and processed cocaine, recreational users began to snort coke (cocaine hydrochloride) in the early part of this century. Gradually, the federal government began to regulate cocaine as a dangerous narcotic. Because of its expense, cocaine was not popular until the late 1960s, when a growing middle class with disposable income discovered the drug. However, in the later 1970s freebasing—preparing coke for injecting or snorting—became popular, and crack (also known as rock) was invented. The price of cocaine plummeted, and it became the Brat Pack drug of choice. Now, crack and cocaine are both readily available, but crack is still regarded as a ghetto drug and often treated differently. (Federal law treats 500 grams of cocaine the same as 5 grams of crack. A gram of coke results in 0.90 grams of crack.)

States That Have Harsher Penalties for Crack than for Cocaine
Connecticut ● Iowa ● Maine ● Maryland ● New Hampshire ● North Dakota ● Ohio ● Oklahoma ● South Carolina ● Wyoming

A CLASSIC: Does Coca-Cola contain cocaine? Not exactly. At the turn of the century, when cocaine was being prescribed as a medication, soft drink manufacturers created a medicinal drink that contained extracts from coco leaves and kola nuts. The kola supplied caffeine, and the coco supplied trace amounts of cocaine for a mildly stimulating drink. When concerns about cocaine abuse came to light, all of the cocaine was removed from the product. Now cocaine free, Coca-Cola still uses coco leaves in its formula. (The recipe is a secret, but other ingredients are sugar, orange oil, lemon oil, and vanilla.) The leaves are processed in only one plant in New York, because it's a felony to process the leaves somewhere else. Where do the leaves grow? Unclear—imported, perhaps?

Facts

Appearance: Cocaine is a fine white powder. Crack is usually off-white or yellow and is a lumpy, chalky substance, sort of a cross between sugar cubes and wax.

Accessories: Mirror (to put coke on), razor blade (to make lines), straws or rolled-up dollar bills. Foil, glass pipe, or flame for crack. Someone to listen to your babble.

Dosage: Difficult to ascertain. Coke is sold in eightballs, about 3.5 grams. A standard line of coke is anywhere from fifty to seventy milligrams of powder. That's the length of a man's thumb and the width of two tooth-picks—approximately. A few (one to four) lines is enough. As for crack, the smaller the rock, the better—you won't need more than one hit. Rocks are usually 0.10 to 0.50 grams each.

Chemical makeup: Eightballs are usually only 25 to 60 percent cocaine—the rest is additives such as baking soda or baby powder. Crack is 70 to 90 percent pure cocaine and usually made with baking soda.

Method of ingestion: Coke: lines of coke snorted through a straw or rolled-up dollar bills. Can be injected (twenty milligrams can kill you this way), rubbed on teeth or gums, or inhaled in nasal spray. Crack: smoked in glass pipes or vaporized on foil over a low flame.

Buzz begins: Snorting: within a minute. Injecting or smok-ing: instantaneous.

Type of buzz: Hyper. Energy, confidence, and invulnerabil-ity to the world's puny problems. Sexual arousal. Euphoria.

Buzz duration: Cocaine lasts for less than thirty minutes. Crack wears off in two to seven minutes.

Negative effects: Sinus problems, nosebleeds, and a nasal drip in the back of your throat from snorting. Comedown will leave you depressed, headachy, lethargic. At high doses, coke can lead to aggressive behavior, paranoia, restlessness, hyperactivity, and increased heart rate and blood pressure. If you do too much, you run the risk of seizures, strokes, heart attacks, and yes, death.

Tolerance: You'll become tolerant to the drug quickly. If you're a heavy user, you'll need to do a lot (you'll probably plateau at some level). Cocaine is addictive—at the very least, psychologically addictive. One line will never seem to be enough. (C'mon, your high won't even last an hour!) Crack is even more addictive.

Penalties for Possession For a narcotic that everyone counts as a "hard" drug, cocaine is often treated with kid gloves. For one thing, cocaine is a Schedule II drug on the federal scale, and on most state scales. That means that the government recognizes that it has some therapeutic use. Cocaine penalties vary wildly, with maximum sentences as low as one year and as high as fifteen years for first-time low-level possession.

Chart 6: Cocaine Penalties

City	Maximum Fine	Maximum Jail Time
Los Angeles (any amount)	Diversion/$20,000	Diversion/ 1.5–3 years
District of Columbia (amount not specified)	$1,000	Up to 6 months
Miami (up to 28 grams)	$5,000	Up to 5 years

City	Maximum Fine	Maximum Jail Time
Chicago (up to 15 grams)	$25,000	1–3 years
Las Vegas (up to 4 grams)	$5,000	1–4 years
New York (up to 0.5 gram)	$1,000	Up to 1 year
Dallas (up to 1 gram)	$10,000	180 days to 2 years

Heroin

Once used in seedy, glamorous opium dens, this product of poppies now has a less fabulous existence in the syringes of addicts. Back in the nineteenth century, opium accompanied Chinese immigrants to Europe and America, and in some places opium dens were as popular as ordinary saloons. Morphine, a derivative from opium, was touted as a cure for alcoholism (and cocaine was used as an antidote for morphine addiction). At the turn of the century, doctors came up with heroin, which many claimed was a safer type of morphine. That, and the invention of the syringe around the same time, have ensured that there have been heroin addicts ever since. By the time heroin was made illegal in 1920, hundreds of thousands of heroin addicts lived all over the country. Those who go into treatment are often given methadone, a synthetic version of heroin, to help lessen their cravings.

Facts

Appearance: Pure heroin is a white, odorless powder like flour. Street colors vary from off-white to brown to black

(black tar—sticky, for smoking). Methadone comes in pills or a liquid that looks like green Kool-Aid.

Accessories: You won't want anything. Literally.

Dosage: Five to ten milligrams injected, five to fifteen milligrams snorted. Heroin is usually sold in hundred-milligram bags. Purity varies greatly.

Chemical makeup: That bag mostly contains other types of powder. However, the potency is getting stronger. In the past, bag would be about 10 percent pure heroin. Now you can get bag with up to 98 percent pure heroin. Additives can be anything.

Method of ingestion: Snorting (common), injecting (traditional), smoking like crack.

Buzz begins: Ten seconds if injected into a vein. Ten to fifteen minutes when snorted.

Type of buzz: Nothingness. After brief orgasmic peak, a feeling of security and numbness. You won't care about anything.

Buzz duration: Three to four hours. You'll peak within ten minutes of ingestion.

Negative effects: Collapsed veins, heart problems, lack of appetite, respiratory problems, abscesses. Withdrawal produces sweating, cramps, diarrhea, shakes, or vomiting. Overdose or injection of impure additives can kill you instantly. And shared needles can transmit diseases.

Tolerance: Very addictive. Your body becomes tolerant almost the first time you do it.

Penalties for Possession Meth and ecstasy might be trendy, but heroin is forever. Usually the province of hard-core junkies, heroin possession has been harshly punished in virtually every state.

Chart 7: Heroin Penalties

City	Maximum Fine	Maximum Jail Time
Los Angeles (any amount)	Diversion/$20,000	Diversion/ 1.5–3 years
District of Columbia (amount not specified)	$1,000	6 months
Miami (up to 4 grams)	$5,000	5 years
Chicago (less than 15 grams)	$25,000	1–3 years
Las Vegas (up to 4 grams)	$5,000	1–4 years
New York (up to 3.1 grams)	$1,000	1 year
Dallas (less than 1 gram)	$10,000	180 days to 2 years

OTHER DRUGS

The truth? The above contraband descriptions barely scratch the surface. Many, many other substances will get you high . . . and possibly in legal trouble.

Drug	Description
Ketamine (K, Special K, Vitamin K)	An animal tranquilizer that produces a dreamy, sleepy, often dissociated effect when injected or snorted
GHB (gamma hydroxybutyrate)	Looks like water. Though it produces effects like alcohol

Drug	Description
	(decreased inhibitions, relaxation, grogginess, dizziness), it should never be mixed with alcohol
Rohypnol	A depressant, also known as the date rape drug
Peyote/Mescaline	A cactus. The mescaline in peyote causes heightened awareness, increased sensory activity, and feelings of intoxication . . . it even has its own religion
PCP (phencyclidine)	A powder that is rumored to make you really strong—and really crazy—at the same time
Nitrous Oxide	Once the sole province of dentists . . . now the short high (often sold in "whippets") is actually legal in many areas

These drugs are not as widely used as the ones described earlier, and their use varies depending on what part of the country you're in.

Reservations Only, Please: Twenty-eight states have passed laws enabling Native Americans to use peyote in "bona fide" religious ceremonies. Twenty-two states have not. The American Indian Religious Freedom Act of 1994 was amended to ensure that Native Americans were not penalized for their use of peyote in religious ceremonies.

There's even the stuff under your kitchen sink—or, as more commonly known, Ways to Get High When You've Run out of Ideas. Nail polish remover, rubber cement, paint thinner, glue, hair spray, lighter fluid, and even helium from balloons have all been used by someone to get high. These items, when used as inhalants, have not been studied, have a variety of untested ingredients, and can even kill with the first dose. They're also legal. If there's any way to recreationally sniff stuff like the Freon from air conditioners—without significant side effects— then nobody knows about it.

MORE PRODUCTS OF AMERICA'S HIGH SCHOOLS: These guys win the Slow Even for Stoners prize. "Harpo," "Groucho," "Chico," and "Zeppo"—all under the age of twenty—are suspected of seventeen burglaries of doctors' and dentists' offices all over Indiana. Looking for OxyContin, a powerful, popular painkiller that produces a heroinlike high, these geniuses grabbed Oxytocin from a vet's office. Sadly, the two drugs are not related, as Oxytocin is given to animals to stimulate lactation and milk production, induce labor, and encourage mothering instincts. Amused law enforcement officials kept an eye on the boys in case they'd actually done the drug instead of selling it.

WHAT IS POSSESSION?

The number one question for the cocktail-party lawyer is "How much can I get away with before I'm in *real* trouble?" Well, what you need to remember about being busted for possession—or anything—is this: an arrest is one thing, but having the case hold up in court is another.

Cops don't need a winning case to bust you for possession. They don't need to concern themselves with proving possession beyond a reasonable doubt—that's the lawyer's job. All they need is probable cause for an arrest. (See chapter 4 for more information on probable cause.) If the case is weak or you have a good defense, it can get dismissed once you're in court. But, by the time the judge hears the lousy case against you, you've already been arrested, booked, and have probably spent time in jail.

Street Law Concept #5: Contraband
Stuff that's illegal to possess, sell, or transport. Examples: narcotic drugs, counterfeit money, child pornography. Not all drugs are considered contraband.

Actual Possession
That's direct, usually physical contact with the contraband in question. The issue here is control: Are you in control of the substance? Or, more realistically, do the cops have reason to think you are?

Physical Contact If it's in your hand, it's possession. When you're physically holding something, you have control over it. But what if you aren't smoking? Generally, to arrest you, the police need more evidence than that you were just hanging out with your drug-using friends. However, if you're passing a joint in a circle—even if you're not smoking it—you can be busted for possession. A cop can just assume that you're partaking, simply because it's in your hand.

THE OLD-FASHIONED WAY: They've lived apart from society, shunning electricity, telephones, and occasionally each other. Now the Amish have a new problem . . . crystal meth? "Friar Tuck" was stopped by the cops, and a search of his truck (what? no wagon?) revealed plastic bags with crystal meth, as well as marijuana, a scale, and lots of cash. Big deal, right? Well, Tuck is a churchgoing member of a rural Amish community in Iowa and works at his father's sawmill. While Tuck was not charged with intent to supply, a couple other sawmill workers were arrested on meth possession charges as well.

Physical possession doesn't just mean when the stuff is in your hands, though. If you're at a party, and you've just snorted some coke, you could be in the other room and still get busted for possession. How? Residue. If you're a sloppy user and it's on your hands or face, cops could infer possession. Ditto if you've got a pipe with weed residue all over it. One of the easiest ways for a cop to spot a user is when residue is on the user's hands, clothes, or face.

Just in case you're wondering: lack of residue won't prove you innocent. They'll just think you're a neat freak. It'll take a lot of work to prove your innocence when the cops have a pretty compelling case using—well, just their own eyes.

On Your Person It should be pretty obvious that the narcotics don't have to be in your hands for direct physical possession. They can be in your pocket, your shoes, or hidden in your wig for all the cops care. All that counts as possession. In these cases, some culprits have tried using the classic "I didn't know it was there" defense. This one is up to the jury. If you've got a dime bag hidden in a secret pocket in a coat inherited from your mother, good luck. If you borrowed your boyfriend's coat five minutes ago to get warm, then you've got a fighting chance. This also includes instances where you possess something with drugs inside. It could be a box you're delivering, a suitcase you're holding, whatever. Again, if you deny knowledge, it will be up to you to prove it.

Street Law Concept #6: Willful Blindness

When you could have known something through "reasonable inquiry," but chose not to do the work. A prime example is when you deliver mysterious packages to people at an airport. Even if you didn't open one of those packages yourself, you're still responsible if those packages deliver contraband or explode. Moral? Sticking your head in the sand or your fingers in your ears is not a good defense.

Basically, in situations where any idiot would have guessed that drugs were in the package, you lose. If you regularly make deliveries of suspicious parcels for some creepy guy whose beeper is always going off, you're going to have a hard time claiming "I didn't know" it was coke. But sometimes, you can be busted if you were carrying a package for a total stranger and had no reason to suspect it was coke. (This is why airports are always asking if anyone has given you a package to carry onto the plane.) The general rule: if you could have discovered the drugs through casual, reasonable inspection and inquiry, and you chose not to, then your goose is cooked.

Constructive Possession

You're not holding any contraband. You're not even in the same room with it. Hell, it's in another part of town. Can you still get busted for possession? Definitely.

Street Law Concept #7: Constructive Possession

When you have "dominion and control" over something, but not actual, physical possession of it. You usually need to have the intent to control the object in question, so if you honestly didn't know it was there, you may not be constructively possessing. But the cops can infer that you had the intent to possess, depending on the circumstances and evidence.

Dominion and control is one of those funky, annoying phrases that can drive nonlawyers crazy. Let's just shorten it to control, only without the physical element. You're not holding it or carrying it on your person, yet you still have control over the substance. Examples?

Your House If the cops find drugs in your house, they can infer that you have control—even if your surfer buddies brought it, or your sister's loser boyfriend hid his stash in your closet. Since you're the one living there, you're responsible for everything that goes on inside.

But, you're thinking, don't the cops need a warrant to search my place? I thought I'd be safe if I smoked it in the privacy of my home! Well, yes and no. The cops usually do need a warrant to search your place. However, there's the Plain View Rule.

> **Street Law Concept #8: Plain View**
>
> An object is in plain view when a cop can see it with his own eyes, or, in certain cases, with a flashlight (if it's dark). He can sometimes use binoculars, but not X-ray equipment or high-tech stuff like that. A Ziploc bag of dope is in plain view when it's on your coffee table. It's not in plain view when hidden in the back of Grandma's closet. When it's in plain view, a cop doesn't need a warrant to seize the evidence.

If your annoying neighbor calls in a noise complaint, the cops can knock on your door and ask permission to look around. Even though the complaint was about the noise, a cop can immediately bust you for possession if you have a hot, resin-filled pipe lying in plain view on the coffee table. And yes, you can be busted for possession for the same pipe even if you're not at home when the cops show up. If you don't know who or what's in your house, then you're asking for trouble.

The Roommate Exception Of course, as with most things, there are exceptions. Primarily, the Roommate Exception (note: this is not a legal term). What if you share a room with someone—like in a dorm? The cops can suspect you of having dominion and control over the drugs in a shared room—for example, if it was in your dresser, not hers. What if (as is more common) you don't share a room? Cops are more likely to infer that you had control if it's in your room, rather than in your roommate's . . . usually. If it's in the common area (living room, bathroom), well, that's up to the officer. He can arrest both of you, neither of you, or one of you. Will the case hold up? Depends on the circumstances (your prior convictions, any para-phernalia found, witness testimony, etc).

The Roommate Exception can help or hurt you, depending on the circumstances. The closer your rela-tionship with the alleged drug user/dealer, the more likely it is that the court will find that you participated in the illicit activity.

STILL LOOKING FOR A FEW GOOD MEN: They say love is blind, but the law ain't. "Catherine of Aragon" was busted in her car for possession with intent to distribute—and one of the determining factors was that she was married to the driver of the car. (The car was hers, too.) Similarly, "Anne Boleyn" was convicted of constructive posses-sion, and the court was allowed to take into account her long-term, live-in relationship with the defendant (who was busted for actual possession).

Note that the case for constructive possession doesn't just include furniture. If the contraband was in your coat pocket, and your coat is in your closet, then the cops can bust you for possession. You have control over your coat, don't you? And if you have a safe-deposit box in the bank filled with weed, you're going down. Whose name is the box registered under? Who else has the key to the box—and therefore control over the weed? You, baby, you.

ONE POTATO, TWO POTATO: Your drugs ain't no hot potato. "Mr. Lucky" thought he'd got off scot-free when he handed off his coke to accomplices in a parking lot. His accomplices were nabbed, and Mr. Lucky was charged with possession under the constructive possession theory. Since the cops never saw Mr. Lucky actually physically possessing the drugs, the grand jury threw out the case. However, an appellate court reinstated the charge, stating that the evidence showed that Mr. Lucky had "dominion and control" over his accomplices, who were merely couriers to Mr. Lucky's customers.

Your Party Any party has its share of crashers. Whether you live in a tiny Manhattan apartment or a sprawling San Diego beach house, you've encountered a situation where, looking around the living room, you think, "Who the hell are these people?" A few strangers can liven up any party, but do you want to be responsible for the coke that they leave behind in your medicine cabinet? Because you probably will be. During the party, you're generally responsible for what goes on in your house. This doesn't mean you'll always get busted for your guests' drugs—especially if they don't tell you they're using or are being so discreet that you don't know about it. However, if the cops show up, and the place reeks of weed, with fragments of coke all over the dinner table, they can start making inquiries. And if the inquiries lead to arrests, chances are the cops will infer that you had "dominion and control" over the drugs in your house.

Remember, once the cops show up, they can stick around if they feel that there's something fishy going on. And just so you don't get the wrong idea, you're not free and clear just because you're a guest, rather than the host.

WRONG TIME FOR A HOUSE CALL: Sometimes it helps to call ahead. "Larry," of Fairbanks, Alaska, arrived at his local crack house, where he was met at the door by police, who were in the middle of a bust. A search of Larry revealed two bundles of cocaine. A little while later, "Moe" knocked on the door and was invited in by the cops, who discovered three crack pipes. Before the officers could catch their breath, "Curly" arrived. The cops searched her, too, finding a glass pipe with coke traces. All three were booked for possession. On appeal, they argued that because they were either invited in by the cops after the search had started or searched in the enclosed porch (an "arctic entry"), the charges should be dismissed. The appellate court wasn't buying it—it held that the warrant included the arctic entry, and that because the warrant was for a type of goods (drugs), rather than one specific item (a ring), the cops were authorized to search anyone who arrived after they did.

Your Car It's pretty much the same story if the drugs are in your car. Just remember the Plain View Rule from the section above. If you get pulled over for a traffic ticket, and the cop spots some bud (or smells a lot of smoke), then he can investigate further and bust you for the weed, no matter what he pulled you over for initially.

It always depends on what state you're in, but if the car is yours, there's generally a "rebuttable presumption" that you're in possession.

Street Law Concept #9: Rebuttable Presumption

A set of facts that the law assumes to be true. It's your job to provide evidence to the contrary. A prime example is the vehicular rebuttable presumption: anything found in the backseat of the car belongs to either the owner or the driver of the car. You can then provide evidence to the contrary.

CAR FOR SALE, POT FOR FREE: "Tom" thought he'd made the deal of a lifetime when he bought a 1987 Nissan Pathfinder for only $2,600 at a federal forfeiture sale in 2001. One year later, while driving in Mexico, Tom and his buddy "Jerry" were stopped by local authorities at a checkpoint. A search of the car turned up a total of seventeen kilos of marijuana (37.4 pounds). Tom and Jerry argued that the pot had come with the car—the former owner, "Bulldog," had lost the Pathfinder after Customs agents found twenty-seven kilos of weed in the gas tank. The Mexican government rejected the argument and threw Tom and Jerry in jail. Their reasoning? Despite testimony that the pot was extremely old and decayed, U.S. Customs officials couldn't possibly have missed the pot a year earlier . . . right? In 2003, a year after their arrest, a federal appeals panel in Mexicali freed the two men, who had spent the time in a bare-bones jail where even visitors had strip searches. Moral? Never trust a "great deal" from the U.S. government.

Possession in Public

You're likely to get into more trouble if you smoke pot on the street rather than in the privacy of your home. In many states, smoking pot on the street can get you a misdemeanor, while smoking pot at home results in a mere violation. This isn't true of every state, but, clearly, where and how you do the drugs can be an important factor in your arrest and punishment.

You might be wondering if your car is considered public. Well, that depends on where your car is—in your garage, in your driveway, on the exit ramp of the freeway?

A lot of special rules apply to cars. For safety's sake, just assume that once you've left the house, you're no longer master of your domain.

Possession in Schools
Virtually every state has harsher penalties for adults (and sometimes juveniles) found with contraband on or near school property. What constitutes "near"? It varies, but most states have a set distance, such as a thousand feet. The penalties often get nastier depending on the level of the school—that is, nastier if you were caught near a middle school rather than a high school, and worse still if you're near an elementary school.

PERSONAL USE VS. SUPPLYING
Let's make it clear, so there's no confusion. Selling or supplying drugs is far more serious than mere possession. This is where you're entering felony territory and could end up with serious prison time.

First—some basics:

Street Law Concept #10: Possession/Possession with Intent/Sale

- Possession: You are actually or constructively possessing the contraband, and it's intended for personal use—usually a small amount.
- Possession with Intent to Sell: Any amount, which you've somehow indicated is for sale.
- Attempt to Sell/Sale: You've just exchanged or tried to exchange your contraband for money, or something else of value.

Street Law Concept #11: Personal Use

Something is for personal use when you're planning to use it. You and no one else. No sharing. Generally, the larger the amount, the less likely the cops are to believe it's just for personal use.

The sale of drugs is no joke. Look at the difference in penalties.

Possession and Sale (1 ounce of marijuana)

	MAXIMUM FINE/TIME FOR POSSESSION	MAXIMUM FINE/TIME FOR SUPPLYING
Los Angeles	$100/no time	Not listed/2–4 years
District of Columbia	$1,000/up to 6 months	$10,000/up to 1 year
Miami	$5,000/up to 5 years	$5,000/up to 5 years
Chicago	$2,500/up to 1 year	$25,000/1–3 years
Las Vegas	$600/no time, probation	$20,000/1–6 years
New York	$500/probably probation	$5,000/up to 4 years
Dallas	$2,000/up to 6 months	$10,000/6 months to 2 years

As you can see by the chart, many states have minimum prison time for dealers—even low-level pot dealers. So it should be pretty obvious that drug dealing is a risky business that can be hazardous not only to your health, but to your freedom.

Of course, it's equally important to make sure that, if you're not dealing, you aren't mistaken for a dealer. Anyone can be busted as a dealer these days—not just the guys in flashy suits and expensive cars. And you don't need to be actively selling anything. Cops—and judges—can infer that just by your stash and your actions. For example, one of the things that cops look for is quantity. It's going to be hard to convince a judge or a jury that your three bricks of coke were solely for personal use. Basically, you can argue till the cows come home, but if there's enough evidence to indicate that you're a seller, you'll be busted as one.

There's basically no gray area here. If you sell your one extra ecstasy pill to your buddy, you're still selling. It doesn't matter to a cop if you just "picked up" an extra pill from your dealer and consider yourself just a courier. It doesn't matter that it's just one pill. If a cop sees you exchange the pill for money—or has enough evidence to know that's what you're doing—then you're a supplier. Period.

I LOST MY HEART IN BUFFALO: When your bags get mixed up at the airport, it's a real bummer. You never know what you'll end up with. Just ask "Pocahontas." When she went to the Delta Airlines counter at Buffalo Niagara International Airport, she was just trying to recover her shipment of weed—all 119 pounds of it. What she ended up with was two boxes of human heart parts. You read that right. Pocahontas ended up with a pulmonary valve headed for an emergency transplant, and a vein intended for coronary bypass surgery. A confused and grossed-out Pocahontas tried to do the right thing—she went back to return the packages (and incidentally, get her pot). Unfortunately, this is when the cops caught her and her partner, charging them both with conspiracy to possess with intent to distribute. (The volume of the haul probably got the "intent to distribute" charge.) Incidentally, the organs made it safely to their surgeries.

The truth is, you'll be more likely to be mistaken for a supplier if you hang around suppliers. Courts will use that as evidence that you're a dealer yourself. Of course, since the eighties ended, it's gotten harder to spot a dealer—the stereotype of the ponytailed, gold-chained drug lord died with the last episode of *Miami Vice*. If you can't tell which of your friends are dealing, and who's just partaking, here's our handy—though slightly tongue-in-cheek—guide.

How to Spot a Dealer

PERSONAL USER	SUPPLIER
Has a modest amount of cash —if any	Has a large amount of cash, organized by bills, usually in rolls
Stoned	Not stoned
Keeps stash in sandwich bag	Divides stash evenly into multiple bags, sometimes marked and labeled
Minimal amount of drugs; most of it at home	large amount of drugs organized as above, often on his person

PERSONAL USER	SUPPLIER
Usually unarmed	Either armed or hanging around with people who are armed
Typical paraphernalia: pipe	Typical paraphernalia: digital scale

X CRACK FOR Y DOLLARS?: "Romulus" and "Remus" not only sold real drugs, they sold fake crack ("flex") to dumber customers. Their attempt to sell $8,000 worth of flex to undercover cops failed, and they were busted. Remember how your sentence gets worse with the more drugs you possess/sell? Well, federal courts are allowed to convert drug money into drug value, if the prosecution shows that the money would go back into drugs anyway. So the federal court in North Carolina held the dynamic duo responsible for all their drug deals, then increased the quantity by $8,000—the value of the flex. However, a higher court noted that some of the flex money was used on legitimate things, and the prosecution had failed to prove that *all* the flex money went back into drug deals.

You especially creative types might have a new question: "Can I make a living selling flex?" Sure, if you're really big or a fast runner. You probably won't be busted for dealing if you put together a wax/flour mixture and knowingly pass it off as crack. (Actually, it's probably fraud, but who's going to report you—the guy trying to buy drugs? Unlikely.) There is, however, one little detail: you have to know it's fake. If you buy, sell, or possess flex and you think it's actually crack, then you're guilty of the attempted purchase, sale, or possession of crack, even though you never had any on you.

FOOL ME ONCE, SHAME ON ME: How do you prove that you knew your crack was fake? "Sherlock Holmes" had that exact problem. During a sting, he made a drug deal with undercover Feds, but sold them procaine instead of coke. As he set up the second deal, he was busted, but the coke was never recovered. At trial, Sherlock claimed that he never intended to sell coke— just more procaine, which is a legal substance. The courts found that since he had knowingly sold fake coke once, he might intend to sell fake coke again. Therefore, the government couldn't prove their case against Sherlock beyond a reasonable doubt. The case left open whether it's a good idea to try to bamboozle the Feds.

Frankly, it's really hard to weasel out of a supply charge through a legal loophole. Many states have fines for mere gifting or delivery of narcotics—even if you didn't receive money or were just delivering for a friend. Penalties also increase if you are a minor, selling to a minor, or are anywhere near school grounds. In even first offenses, selling is almost always a felony.

THE RULES OF PARAPHERNALIA

Ah, paraphernalia. So integral to drug use. So hard to spell. First things first: What exactly is it?

Street Law Concept #12: Paraphernalia

Any object that helps you either (1) do drugs or (2) sell or distribute drugs. It does not matter if the object was originally made to be used as paraphernalia. Any object with residue of narcotics is automatically considered paraphernalia.

The following items are considered paraphernalia whether they are brand-new or have been used for years—and whether you buy them at your local head shop (shop that sells paraphernalia) or make them yourself.

USER PARAPHERNALIA

- Pipes (metal, wood, ceramic, whatever) with or without screens, carbs (holes poked in the sides of the pipe), or punctured bowls
- Gas masks altered for smoking purposes
- Water pipes
- Bongs
- Freebasing cocaine kits
- Roach clips
- Any normal item that has been altered to hide drugs or aid in the ingestion of drugs
- Electric, ice, carb, or chamber pipes
- Syringes and hypodermic needles

DEALER PARAPHERNALIA

- Miniature spoons that are designed to measure one tenth of a cubic centimeter or less
- Small digital scales
- Any normal item that has been altered to either (a) measure quantities of drugs or (b) transport large quantities of drugs
- Items used to cut or dilute raw narcotics

Items such as Baggies, vials, or rolling papers can be construed as paraphernalia depending on the circumstances, but since they have legal uses, they're evaluated case by case. Ditto for items meant for the smoking of tobacco (hookahs, or Grandpa's corncob pipe, for example).

NEEDLE IN A HAYSTACK: Syringe law is a little strange. In fourteen states, you must have a prescription to possess a syringe (unless you're injecting insulin). Ten states require that you provide a written promise that the syringe will be used for a lawful purpose. However, given the dangers of shared needles, many states have exempted syringes from paraphernalia laws. Most states have needle exchange programs—many with public funding. But you're still busted in most states if your syringe has trace amounts of heroin.

Just because you've got some wacky item and you don't see it on the list, don't think you're free and clear. Any item with drug residue—indicating that it has been used to do or deal illegal drugs—can get you busted. Even items that aren't meant to be used as paraphernalia will be treated as such if there's residue of a controlled substance. So your apple bong can get you in as much trouble as that expensive bong sold in your local head shop.

There's no doubt about it: paraphernalia law can be confusing. Consider this head-scratcher: there's no federal law against possessing paraphernalia. That's right—there's nothing technically illegal (under federal law) about owning a bong or a pipe. Federal law prohibits you from selling, importing, or exporting paraphernalia, or using the mail to transport it. But there's nothing on the books about possessing a clean pipe or a bong (clean = no residue whatsoever). You can use it to smoke tobacco or use it as a flower vase. Just no narcotics.

However, get this: most states have laws against possessing paraphernalia even if there's no residue. (Most, but not all: for example, California and New York have laws against paraphernalia, but Wyoming and Oklahoma don't.) If your state doesn't prohibit it, the city or county might have a local ordinance. However, it's usually the residue that gets you in real trouble, even when there are state laws to the contrary.

THE LONG HAUL: Some people travel with their stash. Others seem to take along every drug they've got. Brothers "Jesse James" and "Frank James" were riding high (literally) with buddy "Billy the Kid" when they were pulled over for a routine traffic stop. The smell of marijuana made the cops suspicious, and the cops found some bags in plain view that eventually tested positive for marijuana. The cops searched the three would-be outlaws individually, discovering over $7,000, hundreds of pills, a bag of THC, and four bags of weed. When the cops searched the car, they found the following giant haul: four huge bags of weed, a digital scale, 124 plastic bags, various paraphernalia, and numerous other bags containing pot. Because of the amount of contraband (and the scale and the bags), the three men were charged with multiple counts of drug possession, including the intent to use drug paraphernalia, and criminal conspiracy to manufacture drugs.

Some neighborhoods have head shops; in other cases, a dealer might supply paraphernalia. But now there's the World Wide Web, where you can buy virtually any item of drug paraphernalia quickly and easily and have it delivered neatly to your door in a nice brown-paper-wrapped package. This sort of thing is precisely what the government wants to stop. In Operation Pipe Dreams, Ashcroft and the DEA are methodically targeting Web sites—as well as suppliers and manufacturers—dealing in paraphernalia. This drives prices up and makes paraphernalia dealers more cautious about whom they sell to.

> **THE END OF AN ERA:** First Cheech Marin got stuck on the show with Don Johnson. Then Tommy Chong gets busted by the Feds. Chong's likeness appeared on a variety of glass paraphernalia, including bongs, and he had invested nearly $300,000 in the industry. Then one day he signed a bong for a pair of undercover agents in a Texas head shop. Busted, Chong pleaded guilty. Federal sentencing guidelines require a six-to-twelve-month term, proving that an aging hippie is no match for thousands of heavily armed DEA officers.

OTHER ISSUES YOU'RE WONDERING ABOUT
Here's some general information about some common issues that might crop up for you and your amigos.

Medicinal Marijuana
From Woody Harrelson to the folks at the NORML (National Organization for the Reform of Marijuana Laws), a whole host of smokers, politicians, and average folks believe that marijuana should be legalized. Some think it's just a harmless substance; others are more impressed by its medicinal value. Currently, thirty-five states have laws that allow marijuana possession in some form, in some circumstances. But weed advocates have a long way to go.

What are the medical uses of marijuana, you ask? (And how can I qualify?) For some patients, marijuana can relieve nausea and chronic muscle aches without severe side effects. It can be used to treat the symptoms of a host of diseases, including AIDS and cancer. However, two things stand in the way of you going out and getting a prescription for weed: (1) it's not always easy to qualify as a medicinal marijuana patient, and (2) even if the state you live in legalized pot for sale at your local deli, the Feds still consider both the supply and the possession of weed for *any* reason illegal.

What does that mean? Well, state laws do not have to be the same as federal laws. That means that if you, as a medicinal marijuana patient in California, grow and use your own weed for medicinal purposes (but don't sell it to others), you are safe from state prosecution. However, you're still subject to the U.S. government coming in and prosecuting you at a federal level.

ONE SMALL STEP: The federal government, in general, is pretty intolerant of marijuana use, but the Ninth Circuit Court recently upheld the rights of two seriously ill women who possessed medicinal marijuana. The court stated that since the women smoked for medical reasons, and the stash was clearly for private use, it didn't affect interstate commerce and was therefore not drug trafficking. The Bush administration asked the court to change its mind, but the judges denied the request, standing by their original decision. The Ninth Circuit encompasses the states of Alaska, Arizona, Hawaii, Nevada, Oregon, and Washington— all of which have medicinal marijuana laws.

In general, the Feds are usually too busy to bust lone medicinal marijuana patients. But think about this: What if you didn't grow your own? So then you do what you'd do for any product, right? You buy it from a distributor. Unfortunately, these distributors (often known as cannabis buyers' clubs) get busted regularly by the Feds—even though state law allows them to operate. When their prosecution stalls or after they pay their fees, they open up again—only to get busted again. This sort of legal merry-go-round happens regularly in legalized-marijuana states, generally confusing and frustrating everyone. The only people getting happy are the lawyers—these cases can be appealed and go on for years.

Say this doesn't dissuade you—you still want your pot. You should also know that medicinal marijuana laws come in a variety of forms:

Decriminalized These states have *decriminalized* pot at the state level. That means you can grow, cultivate, and use marijuana for medicinal purposes at the state level. There are limits to amounts, you always need a doctor's approval, and it must be for personal use only.

Street Law Concept #13: Decriminalization Versus Legalization

● Decriminalization: The action is not considered criminal. Usually legislation is adopted to "decriminalize" an activity, or the law making something illegal is repealed.
  Though the activity will no longer be punished, there aren't any laws or guidelines for it.
● Legalization: The activity in question is declared to be legal. Generally, the community will start enacting standards and laws to govern and protect the activity.

Only in the Lab Twenty-six states allow patients to use medicinal marijuana only through state-run research programs. Unfortunately, most of these programs ceased to operate in the eighties. Even if they were to get funded again, these programs are extremely rare and hard to get into. Generally, though, these states will be able to provide more information on medicinal marijuana than others.

Just Words These states like to tease their constituents. Some states allow medical marijuana through a doctor's prescription—only it's illegal to prescribe marijuana in those states. Others allow the state to dispense confiscated marijuana—only no state government would dare to do it. These and other states recognize marijuana's therapeutic use, but they're not really going to back up that thought with actions. Yet.

Medicinal Marijuana Laws

DECRIMINALIZED POT	RESEARCH PROGRAMS
Alaska	California
Arizona	Georgia
California	Michigan
Colorado	New Mexico
Hawaii	New York
Maine	Tennessee
Nevada	Washington
Oregon	
Washington	

No matter what your situation is, you need a doctor to officially recommend pot for you (usually, she can't officially prescribe it). You need to show that you have a specific ailment or disease that is treatable with marijuana, and that you only possess enough for personal use. Each state has slightly different requirements, and to qualify, participants need to follow them to the very last letter.

Rules for Medicinal Marijuana

1. Know the maximum number of plants or maximum number of ounces you're allowed to have at one time, and stick to it. If you've got too much, it becomes harder to argue that it's for personal use.
2. Find your doctor through referrals or through cannabis growers' clubs. Try to test their views about medicinal marijuana by asking questions rather than demanding a pot prescription outright. Many doctors will encourage you to seek more conventional medical alternatives to pot.
3. Make sure your illness is one that the state recognizes as being treatable by marijuana.
4. Keep copies of your prescription. In some states, a doctor can't prescribe marijuana, but they can recommend it on a more unofficial level. Get it in writing.
5. If the police show up at your door, show them your prescription and your doctor's contact information.
6. Some states protect a "primary caregiver" who grows marijuana for the patient. Some don't. Know whose growing rights are protected.

Drug Tests

The litigation about when and where drug testing is legal goes back a long way, and there aren't many hard-and-fast rules. You can complain all you want about your privacy and the Fourth Amendment, but the government—and the Supreme Court—isn't afraid to say that drug testing is perfectly fine . . . in certain circumstances.

Street Law Concept #14: Fourth Amendment Primer
The Fourth Amendment protects you against unreasonable searches and seizures. This includes searches of your home, your car, and your body. Drug tests are considered searches and must not violate the Fourth Amendment.

Still in High School? Forget about it. Everyone is worried about drugs in school, and as minors, you have less of a right to privacy than adults do. There's a "compelling interest" for drug tests in schools (much like locker searches) and it's not getting any better.

DRUG TESTS: NOT JUST FOR ATHLETES ANYMORE: In 2002, the Supreme Court okayed an Oklahoma school district's plan to drug test every student who wanted to be involved in *any* extracurricular activity—including those in the chess club (those steroid freaks!) and the choir (those syringe-happy punks!). The court held that there didn't need to be a particular suspicion of drug activity—in fact, the school didn't need any reason whatsoever.

Job Applicant? Your employer has a right to ask you to take a drug test. In some states, you might have the right to refuse and not lose your chance at the job.

At Work? Your employer may have the right to drug test you while you're working for him. It all depends on the state you're in (and their privacy laws) and what you do.

If you work the copy machine at Kinko's or are an interior decorator, there's nothing in your job that's "safety-sensitive" (the government's phrase, not ours).

Street Law Concept #15: Safety-Sensitive

There are many standards for deciding a job is "safety-sensitive." Generally, if you work with children, with large machinery, in the criminal justice system, or in the realm of public safety, then your job is safety-sensitive. Some high-security government or financial jobs are safety-sensitive as well.

In safety-sensitive jobs, drug testing is more reasonable, more likely, and harder to get out of.

Your employer might be violating privacy laws if he springs a "surprise" drug test on you or your coworkers. Many states prohibit random surprise drug tests without at least some suspicion of a problem (for example, if you had a history of drug abuse or appear intoxicated). Unless your job is safety-sensitive, you can't be subjected to a surprise drug test in these states.

Types of Drug Tests

URINE	HAIR	BLOOD
Cheap and common: the poor man's test. Can possibly be passed if you've abstained for a few weeks. The least intrusive from a Fourth Amendment perspective.	Pricier and less common. Won't be fooled by your recent abstinence.	Rare, expensive, and scarily accurate. Most likely to be a violation of your Fourth Amendment rights. Check local privacy laws.

How to Pass Every Drug Test with Flying Colors, Every Time

Don't take drugs.

Sorry, but that's the only way. The same surefire way to avoid pregnancy is the same way to avoid flunking a drug test: abstinence.

Sure, on the Internet, you'll find hundreds, maybe thousands, of products that claim they can enable you to pass drug tests. Some are herbal, some are chemical. Some come with endorsements, others don't. There's also a lot of advice out there: drink lots of water, call in sick on drug test day, etc. It's up to you whether you want to try these tactics on your employer.

What Do They Test For? Ironically, harder drugs like heroin and coke leave your system a lot earlier than marijuana does. Below is a list of commonly tested-for drugs and how long they tend to stay in your body. Be aware that these times are approximate and depend on your body mass, body fat, and the frequency and amount of your usage.

Drugs and Their Time in Your System

Drug	Length of Time It Stays in Your Body
Marijuana/Hash	3–5 days (onetime, one-hit usage) Up to 90 days (multiple usage)
Cocaine	2–6 days
Ketamine (rarely tested)	2–4 days

Drug	Length of Time It Stays in Your Body
GHB (rarely tested)	6–48 hours
Methamphetamines (crystal meth/speed)	3–5 days
Amphetamines	1–4 days
Heroin	1–4 days
PCP	2–7 days (single use)
	Up to 30 days (habitual use)
Ecstasy	2–7 days
LSD	1–4 days
Mushrooms (psilocybin)	1–6 days
Alcohol	6–24 hours

If You Fail . . . If you fail your drug test, you have some options. Drug tests are not 100 percent reliable, and "false positives" have been known to occur. Also, states have rules regarding drug testing, and your employer should have followed them to the letter. You might also be on medications that show up as narcotics on the drug test. A lot of employers will spring for drug rehab before firing you. If it comes to that, get a lawyer.

Making Your Own

For some frequent consumers of contraband, this might sound like a reasonable idea. Cut out the shady middleman, ensure product quality, reduce the risk of being busted—all in the privacy of your own home. But as tempting as it sounds, the cultivation of drugs is often treated in the same way as a sale of drugs. This includes innocuous marijuana plants; cultivation (without a prescription) is almost always a felony.

> **ARGUMENT FOR DIGITAL CAMERAS:** There are dumb potheads, smart potheads, and then ones who clearly need to cut down. In June of 2003, "Albert Einstein" was so proud of his thriving pot plants that he decided to send photographs to the industry magazine *High Times*. Unfortunately, instead of taking Polaroid shots, the proud gardener sent his roll of film to the local drugstore, complete with his home address on the envelope. Cops busted Einstein and found the weed— and, of course, assorted paraphernalia. Einstein and his green thumb face numerous felony charges.

Organic substances, such as weed or mushrooms, are far easier to cultivate than chemical compounds such as ecstasy and crystal meth. Ecstasy in particular requires lots of time, patience, and chemistry skills. Homegrown cocaine is virtually unheard of—in fact, courts have even made the legal assumption that if you have coke, it orig-inated overseas.

The manufacturing of crystal meth has become more popular in the United States. It takes four separate steps and involves a multitude of paraphernalia and ingredients (drain cleaner, coffee filters, WD-40, muristic acid, rubber tubing, oxygen masks, anhydrous ammonia—just to name a few). There are many environmental hazards; the toxic odors and fumes means even living next to a lab is danger-ous—months after the lab is gone. (Cops often wear gas masks or chemical suits when cleaning up busted labs.) Since meth manufacturing leaves a huge amount of trash and harmful by-products, you can be busted for environmental pollution as well as drug manufacturing.

> **RENTERS BEWARE:** The "Joneses" of Spokane, Washington, rented out their second house with hopes that the renters would pay on time and take care of the place. What they got was a police raid and a SWAT team breaking down the door and arresting their renters. The charge? The renters were running a meth lab. The nightmare continued for the Joneses as they discovered over $26,000 worth of damage, including torn floors, ruined pipes, and the stench of chemical fumes. Insurers were not required to pay for "contamination," and the Joneses were forced to file a suit against their renters to get some of the cleanup costs.

Nice and Legal: Prescription Drugs

Oh, no, you're thinking. Not my medicine cabinet! After all, you've never broken a law in your life, and any drug you take has a prescription from a reputable doctor. So you're in the clear, right?

Well, most of the time, yes. But remember: the federal list of controlled substances includes drugs that are commonly prescribed for medicinal purposes. Just because it's a "legal" drug doesn't mean it's not a controlled substance. Drugs like Valium, Ritalin, and morphine are legal—but you'd better have a prescription for them. In fact, one of the most abused drugs is OxyContin, a legal painkiller sold for high prices on the black market.

Possessing these drugs in enormous quantities or

without a prescription handy can mean a drug possession charge. A prime example of this is the Winona Ryder case. In addition to having sticky fingers in a department store, Ms. Ryder was busted for having a considerable amount of legal prescription drugs—specifically, six different kinds (liquid Demerol, Vicoprofen, Vicodin, Percodan, Valium, and morphine sulfate. Whew!)—and a syringe in her purse. The prescriptions came from different doctors and were prescribed to Ryder under two different names. The drug count was eventually dropped when it was proven that she did, indeed, have prescriptions for the drugs in her possession.

RUSH-ING TO JUDGMENT: He's always been controversial, but 2003 was a banner year for Rush Limbaugh. First the radio show host resigned from his position at ESPN's *Sunday NFL Countdown* amid backlash for his comment that Philadelphia Eagles quarterback Donovan McNabb was "overrated" because fans wanted to see a black quarterback win. A mere month later, Rush ended up confessing to an eight-year addiction to painkillers, most notably OxyContin. Rush, who had started taking pills after back surgery (and, well, just didn't stop), spent five weeks in rehab before returning to his radio show with his usual bluster. Promising not to be a "linguine-spined liberal," the ultraconservative talk show host did not comment on his previous statements that drug addicts should be dealt with harshly by the justice system. The scandal continues, however, as authorities continue to investigate how Rush got over two thousand painkillers from four doctors, and whether money-laundering was involved.

You don't need to treat prescription drugs with the same caution as Schedule I or II drugs, but you still need to be careful when you carry them around. If they're found loose and unidentified in your purse, you could be busted for possession of a controlled substance. Most pharmacies will print the prescription on the bottles they give you, to provide the patient with proof that the medi-cation was legally obtained. When the pills are found outside these bottles, cops have no idea if you have a prescription or not.

And it's not about your traveling stash either. If the police are knocking on your door and your house resembles something out of *Valley of the Dolls,* then you might have to do some fast talking.

Traveling with Your Stash
Have the urge to travel high? Don't.

Crossing state lines with controlled substances can result in federal charges. If you're traveling with a substantial amount, then the cops can assume that you're a drug trafficker. (In fact, they're more likely to jump to this conclusion when you're crossing state lines than when you're sitting around in your house.)

Street Law Concept #16: Interstate Commerce

Any commercial traffic between citizens of different states. Includes transportation and sale of property across state lines, as well as anything mailed. Interstate commerce is governed by federal law and the Feds take it seriously—especially when it comes to the transport of contraband.

Airports and airplanes are governed by federal law and federal marshals. Post 9-11, everyone is looking for secret compartments and hidden pockets. Sure, it's possible that a little weed might just get you a slap on the wrist or even be overlooked. But travel with anything harder and the DEA will definitely show up to whisk you away in the FedMobile.

> **DEALERS ARE PEOPLE, TOO:** Chicago-based drug dealers "Ozzie" and "Rocco" lured Detroit cocaine dealers to Chicago, sold them fake crack, then robbed them of $25,000. Dealers robbing dealers—who cares, right? Well, the Feds did—they busted Ozzie and Rocco for violating the Hobbs Act, which prohibits any action that has a reasonable probability of affecting interstate or foreign commerce. Which was odd, because the commerce in question was drug dealing. "But the crack was fake!" you cry. Well, the courts found that the relevant issue wasn't that the crack was fake, but rather that if the Detroit dealers hadn't been robbed, they might have used the money to buy cocaine somewhere else. Since all cocaine originates overseas, those transactions counted as interstate commerce, and the Ozzie/Rocco robbery had a "reasonable probability" of interfering with that.

As for not driving high—you know all those don't-drink-and-drive warnings? Same deal. Before you try, ask yourself this question: "Do I really want some doped-up driver on the same road as Grandma?" Didn't think so.

Arranging a Sale

You're bragging to your friends about your stash. It's the best pot you've ever had—cheap, fresh, and the high lasts for days. You brag so much your friend says, "Help me out," and asks for the pager number. Should you give it to him? And if you do, could the cops find you guilty of arranging a sale?

Maybe. It depends on what else you do. The first thing you should know is that the charge of arranging a sale is bad news. Even if the sale doesn't go through, you're going to get the same punishment as the supplier.

Though the rules vary from state to state, cops can usually bust you for arranging a sale in one of two ways. They either have a statute against arranging a drug sale, or they'll bust you on a conspiracy charge.

Street Law Concept #17: Conspiracy
A conspiracy occurs when two or more people decide that they're going to do something illegal, then do an overt act to further that illegal action. What's an overt act? Keep reading . . .

Street Law Concept #18: Overt Act
Any outward act that was intended to aid in commiting a crime.

What does this mean for you? Generally, when you simply hand someone a pager number—and that's all you do—you're not conspiring with the dealer to sell drugs. (It's a fine line, but that's generally the case.) That changes, however, if the dealer cuts you in for a finder's fee for getting him another client. Once money's involved, the government looks at you differently. If you appear too knowledgeable about money and pricing, then the cops might infer that you are knowledgeable enough to arrange a sale . . . or have something to gain by the sale going through.

The same goes if you do something other than give your friend the number. What if you call your dealer for your friend because your dealer won't answer a strange page? That could easily be construed as an overt act. Sure, you're just trying to be a good friend, but you're taking an action necessary for the sale to happen. Without you, it probably won't. Any helpful act—from getting a friend a good deal to driving a friend to the dealer's—can be construed as an overt act. You can joke all you want about helping someone connect with a dealer, and you're probably safe, as long as you don't do something.

However, if you offer to hook someone up with some dope and instead take their money and run, you probably won't get busted for arranging a sale. Why? Think about it. You never intended to arrange a sale—just rip the guy off. It's not drug dealing. Fraud, maybe, but not dealing.

CHAIN OF FOOLS: In August 2000, "Garfield" told an undercover cop he had some coke. He named a price, took her money, and told her to "wait there" while he went to get it. Hey, if it walks like a dealer and talks like a dealer, it must be a dealer, right? Not exactly. Since Garfield never actually said that he would make the exchange, and since he had no coke on him when he was busted, the Utah court found that he wasn't guilty of arranging a sale. After all, Garfield could have been planning to run off with the cop's money (never a good idea, by the way). The court stated that Garfield didn't do enough to show that he was "in the chain of distribution," and the police should've waited for Garfield to complete the transaction—or at least get further along.

The more removed you are from the world of drugs and dealers, the less likely you'll be mistaken for a dealer. This is one time that it doesn't pay to be too helpful or too generous. Remember: friends don't let friends become co-conspirators.

Repeat Offender

Some hopeless types can't get their act together and keep getting caught. If you find yourself becoming one of them, then stop using. Really. The high you're getting off your stash is clearly making you stupid. Otherwise you wouldn't be a repeat offender.

Now, many repeat offenders are addicts who can't seem to get clean. Drug addiction, after all, is a disease, and not an easy one to survive. But if you're a recreational, occasional user who doesn't have enough sense to steer clear of the cops, you're doing something wrong. Either your profile is too high or you're careless or you're hanging out in the wrong crowd. Something isn't working, and if you can't figure out what it is, then quit using.

Who can forget poor Robert Downey Jr.? Handsome, famous, rich, charming—yet he spends more time in the slammer than he does on the set.

YES, THEY'RE BETTER THAN YOU AND ME: Or is it you and *I*? In the last few years, Robert Downey Jr. has gotten, broken, and modified his probation so much that everyone has lost track. Eventually, in 1998, Downey was sentenced to six months in jail. Nonetheless, the Superior Court of Los Angeles ordered the sheriff to release him from the county jail so that he could participate in the postproduction of one of his movies. The sheriff opposed the motion, and a higher court noted that this "work release request" was only given upon good cause. Given that jail personnel would've been pulled away for the release, and that "good cause" is usually a funeral, the request was ultimately denied. Would an ordinary guy from the hood have gotten the same treatment? Who knows?

Penalties for all drugs increase exponentially with every offense, and you will soon be facing a mandatory minimum. And if you get busted more than once for dealing, some states have draconian drug laws to keep you incarcerated for years. This includes the sale of marijuana. As far as the government is concerned, you're a menace to society.

CONCLUSION

There are as many ways to get high as there are imaginative people out there trying to find them. Many—including alcohol—are legal. If you resort to illegal methods for a good buzz, then make sure you know what you're doing. It's no fun if the short-term high isn't worth the long-term consequences.

CHAPTER 2

Doing the Nasty: Sex, Nudity, and All That Other Good Stuff

INTRODUCTION

Drug busts are scary, but not everyone does drugs. One way or another, however, virtually everyone is getting laid. And unless you're dating someone who's wearing a locked chastity belt, you've probably been known to engage in at least a small public display of affection or some mild groping. Guess what? The law pokes its head in here, too.

Welcome to the crazy intersection of sex and the law, where a blow job can be a crime, and a lap dance can be considered prostitution. Even weirder is all the stuff you don't think about: Can I have sex with a Halloween pumpkin? Why can't I store a dozen big sex toys in my car? What exactly qualifies as lewd behavior? For some reason, ever since Adam and Eve lost their fig leaves, the law has been interested in regulating sex. We don't know why, but the agenda is clear: anything other than husband-wife sex, preferably in the missionary position, seems to offend somebody.

A blow job may not sound that kinky to you, but as crazy as it may seem, people have gone to jail for getting, giving, and offering blow jobs, even in their own homes. And it just goes downhill from there. Somewhere along the way, sex became a legally suspect activity, with a lot of lawmakers trying to make sure that you do it only in a statutorily authorized way.

SEX AND NUDITY IN PUBLIC PLACES

These days, really safe sex requires a lot more than just a condom—it requires complete privacy. Whenever you engage in sex or masturbation outside your house, you're actually risking an arrest in all fifty states. You might be getting sexy in your backyard or by your open bedroom window, but if your neighbors have an ax to grind, you could get into legal trouble. And just because you're in a public place where the proprietor is encouraging you to let loose doesn't mean you're safe either. If you're determined to bring your sexy antics outside the bedroom, then you'd better know what the law thinks.

Your Home

You own or rent the place, and you know from cop shows that the police need to get a warrant before they can set foot in there. So it should follow that you can fornicate freely in your own home, right?

Well, that's open to some debate. The first thing you need to think about is the show you're giving the neighbors. In other words, shut the blinds. Your neighbors aren't required to ignore your sexual gymnastics, and if they see you and your partner(s) and don't like it, they have every right to call the police.

This is where foreseeability comes in.

> **Street Law Concept #19: Foreseeability**
> An event is foreseeable if the average person of ordinary intelligence could have expected the event to occur. For example, if you drop an egg off a building and it hits a car, then you're responsible for the damage—any average person could have foreseen that the egg might do some damage.

To be private, the sex must be done in a place where it is not "reasonably foreseeable" that anyone could see you. That is, a reasonable person couldn't have guessed that he was being watched.

> **Street Law Concept #20: The Reasonable Person**
> Many legal issues are seen from the point of view of this hypothetical "reasonable person." This is generally the average, ordinary person with average, ordinary intelligence. How the reasonable person acts in the situation in question often decides how the law should rule.

A PUBLIC EXAMPLE: Some people took the apple pie masturbation sequence in *American Pie* a little too seriously. After masturbating in the backyard, "Old MacDonald" of Warren, Michigan, decided that that damn Halloween pumpkin was just too sexy to ignore. Multiple neighbors observed him giving his lucky jack-o-lantern the lay of a lifetime in his basement. Horrified, they called the police, and MacDonald was arrested for indecent exposure and sentenced to ninety days in jail. According to the Michigan Department of Corrections' Web site, Old MacDonald is a habitual criminal and sexual delinquent and was placed in an intensive program for sexual offenders. Among other things, this program forbids him to own any children's clothing or games, go to strip clubs, leave the state, pick up hitchhikers, or go closer than five hundred feet to a school.

Keep in mind that a hidden spot in a public place is still a public place in the eyes of the law. The bushes in the park, the last stall at the men's room, the supply closet at work, behind the Dumpster in the alley—don't fool yourself into thinking they're private just because you think no one can see you. Leave the house ready to engage in some sexual adventure, and you are taking a legal risk. Whether it's worth it or not is up to you . . .

A PRIVATE EXAMPLE: In Pleasant Gap, Pennsylvania, "Flash" presented his neighbors with his unpleasant gap by often gardening nude. The neighbors finally called the cops. Flash was arrested for indecent exposure and sentenced to seven months' probation. However, the conviction was overturned. For one thing, his nosy neighbors were sixty-five yards away, and the court ruled that Flash's backyard was reasonably private. Frustrated Assistant District Attorney Lance Marshall gave up the prosecution but reserved the right to bust Flash in the future for disorderly conduct—essentially reserving his right to remain (ahem) a pain in the ass.

Your Car

Popular British actor Hugh Grant provides some guidance on this important issue. Hugh was busted with a Hollywood hooker named Divine Brown, who was going down on him in the front seat of his car when the bright lights shined. Since the police did not observe any money change hands, Hugh was not busted for solicitation of prostitution, but for lewd conduct in a "public place." Sure, it was his car, but it was by the side of the road. According to Brown, if Hugh had paid another $40, they could have gone to a hotel and avoided that whole encounter with Jay Leno.

And if you have thoughts about fooling around in the back of a cab, you're doing so at your own risk. At the very least, you might get kicked out. In the worst-case scenario, the cab will take you to a police station. Some cabs have video cameras, too, so your amorous encounter might be recorded for posterity . . . or on *America's Funniest Home Videos*.

INDECENT EXPOSURE

Skin. We've gone from a discreetly revealing Victorian ankle to Britney Spears's superstrength thong holding on for dear life. There's a chance, however, that if you expose your "private parts" in a public place with the intent to arouse or gratify the sexual desires of any person, you can be arrested for indecent exposure. This includes situations where you should have known that someone will be alarmed—as opposed to aroused—by your private parts.

What's a Private Part?

Every kid knows what a private part is, right? You would think the lawmakers would, too. But the legal definition of a private part has been the subject of much debate.

> **Street Law Concept #21: Private Parts**
> Though the definitions vary, the anus, genitals, pubic area, and any portion of a woman's nipple are private parts. The ass may be considered a private part, but it depends on the circumstances. Keep reading.

Mooning

The venerable tradition of mooning has been outlawed in public places in all fifty states, much to the chagrin of frat boys everywhere. Though aggravated mooning (spreading your butt cheeks ["brown eyes"], slapping your butt cheeks while mooning, employing inanimate objects, and mooning in highly public areas) is more likely to result in criminal charges, even simple mooning can lead to arrest and jail time.

In many states, just being nude, without sexual intent, won't usually get you arrested for indecent exposure, because you usually have to have a lewd or obscene motivation (like having sex). But don't pull your pants down yet. As you can see from the next examples, there are exceptions. Furthermore, if cops can't arrest your nude self under an indecent exposure statute, you can still get busted for disorderly conduct.

PUTTING THE ASS IN MANASSAS: The city of Manassas, Virginia, lost its sense of humor about private parts after the lurid Lorena Bobbitt trial and has desperately been working to regain its dignity. So when a local radio station held the "Show Your Ass for a Boarding Pass!" contest for a trip to see a Christina Aguilera concert in the Bahamas, the local authorities were not amused. After seeing a photo of station employee

"Dick" with his ass strategically placed in front of the "Welcome to Manassas" sign, prosecutors had both Dick and his accomplice "Jane" arrested for indecent exposure (she took the picture). Both face a year in jail and fines of $2,500.

Streaking—unless you're somehow manipulating your private parts while running—will usually get you the same penalty as mooning.

If you pull down your pants and moon someone, only they can't actually see your ass, are you in trouble? In Michigan, among other states, the answer is yes. It is not necessary for your victim to actually see your ass for you to get busted for mooning. Even if the victim's view of your ass is blocked by a tree, or your victim is too far away, that you've pulled your pants down at all is enough to bust you. Michigan's highest court has held that the crime of indecent exposure is complete when you have intentionally revealed your buttocks, whether someone actually sees them or not.

Thongs

Thong law is fluid. It changes with who's wearing it, how it fits, where it's worn and why. A woman in a thong on the beach is usually not subject to arrest in most states— indecent proposals maybe, but not jail time. On the other hand, a fat man in a thong, pedaling a tricycle past a preschool, is a likely candidate for arrest.

> **INDENT THONG:** Some guys use lines to get a woman's attention. Others take the more direct approach. "Heathcliff" was looking to get his pen refilled at

"Cathy's" office supply store in Virginia. Cathy set about finding a refill, but when she came back, she saw that Heathcliff had dropped his shorts and was wearing only "a real skimpy G-string." This allowed Cathy to get a clear view of the outline of Heathcliff's penis and a tangle of pubic hair. Heathcliff turned slowly around for her, but, alas, left without a phone number. When he returned a week later to see if Cathy had changed her mind, she called the cops. The Virginia Court of Appeals upheld Heathcliff's conviction for indecent exposure, finding that buttocks are a "private part" and that Heathcliff had willfully caused Cathy alarm. The dissent argued that since Heathcliff had not shown his penis or his anus, he had not revealed any of his private parts and that his conviction should be overturned. No such luck.

LEWD CONDUCT

Simply put, lewd conduct is getting it on, with or without a partner, in a public place. You don't have to be nude to be charged with lewd conduct—just ask Bobby Brown, who was busted for lewd conduct for miming a "sexual act" onstage in Atlanta in 1989. Most lewd conduct laws have an intent requirement: you have to be trying to get off, shock someone, or gross someone out.

Street Law Concept #22: Lewd Conduct vs. Indecent Exposure
Lewd conduct centers mostly around sexual acts, real or mimed. You don't actually have to be naked though, as the Bobby Brown case proves. Indecent exposure usually involves nudity, and some sexual or obscene gestures. Lewd conduct usually has tougher penalties.

SEX IN THE CATHOLIC CHURCH? NEVER!: "Beatrice" and her boyfriend "Benedict" were charged with obscenity in the third degree and public lewdness for allegedly having sex in Manhattan's St. Patrick's Cathedral, a few feet away from parishioners. Hey—don't knock it, the radio told them to do it! The couple were attempting to win a contest, sponsored by WNEW-FM and *The Opie and Anthony Show,* which encouraged contestants to have sex in risky places. Producer "Shakespeare" was also arrested, since he was in the cathedral and giving the play-by-play via cell phone. The wise and learned show of disc jockeys Gregg "Opie" Hughes and Anthony Cumia was promptly canceled. Opie and Anthony had previously been fired from a Massachusetts radio station for reporting that the mayor had died in a car crash.

Remember, in some cases, your house can be considered a public place. However, if you're pleasuring yourself in front of the picture windows over your neighbor's yard, you are definitely risking arrest for lewd conduct. The situation might be different if you had no idea—and no reason to think—that you'd be seen. The simple fact is, if you should have known your neighbors could see you, it doesn't matter that you didn't actually know.

Mile High

Ah, the Mile High Club. Somehow, having quick, usually unsatisfying sex in a cramped airplane bathroom can make any guy feel like Hugh Hefner. Who knows why?

Maybe it's the legal danger. Airplanes and airports are governed by federal law, which is pretty unforgiving when it comes to lewd conduct. Furthermore, if you decide to skip the gross bathrooms and do it in your seat, it becomes a felony if a child under sixteen witnesses your shenanigans. In any case, if you're caught, maybe you'll get off with a warning. Then again, maybe you'll get zapped by a federal marshal's stun gun. Who knows?

Chart 8: Lewd Conduct Laws

The chart below will give you an idea of lewd conduct laws. Unless otherwise specified, these laws are not triggered unless the conduct is lewd, lascivious, sexually oriented, or obscene. The chart applies, therefore, if you're having sex in the park, but not necessarily if you're mooning someone. Remember the following, though: (1) the penalties are for first-time offenders and may include fines, jail time, or both; (2) the penalties increase if you knowingly do it with or in front of a minor; and (3) you can always get arrested under a disorderly conduct statute if you're nude but not lewd.

City	Maximum Fine	Jail Time	Other Issues
Los Angeles	$500	6 months	Includes counseling someone to expose themselves. If exposure takes place in an area where offender entered without consent, penalty can go up to 1 year
District of Columbia	$300	90 days	You must be "obscene"—mere nudity is not enough

City	Maximum Fine	Jail Time	Other Issues
Miami	$1,000	1 year	Exposure of sexual organs. Mere nudity without lewdness is not enough
Chicago	$2,500	1 year	Public indecency. Must be lewd
Las Vegas	$2,000	1 year	Penal code contains two separate offenses: indecent exposure and lewd conduct. They have the same penalties
New York	$500	3 months	Mere exposure is a violation. Penalties listed are for lewd exposure
Dallas	$2,000	6 months	*Any* exposure is a Class C misdemeanor

SEX AND NUDITY IN DESIGNATED PUBLIC PLACES

Is the law everywhere? Maybe. Take strip clubs, for example. Even if employees or other patrons of an establishment are encouraging you to whip it out or get it on, you're still subject to arrest if you do. (Exception: nudist colonies and some nude beaches.) The more flesh exposed and the raunchier the behavior in the club, the more likely it is that the police are keeping an eye on the place. And once it's on their radar, it's only a matter of time before they raid the joint and arrest everyone inside.

Strip Clubs

Strip clubs are packed with customers—and sometimes cops—any day of the week, any time of day. As a result, both strip clubs and porn theaters are becoming more and more regulated.

Street Law Concept #23: Strip Club

A strip club is a place where the dancers are at least topless, if not nude in some portion. Most strip clubs offer dances for individuals or groups, in the form of lap, couch, or table dances. It is understood that the dancers will be tipped.

As long as there have been places of ill-repute, there have been legislatures trying to shut them down—and, occasionally, bust the patrons as well. Following a 2000 Supreme Court decision, states are free to ban all nude dancing, so long as the state claims to be trying to address the "harmful secondary effects" of strip clubs—namely, that they attract skuzzy people and all the bad stuff that comes along with them. (If a state were to ban nude dancing without at least claiming it was fending off scuzzy people, it would be a violation of the First Amendment's protection of freedom of expression. And you say the Bill of Rights never did anything for you.)

CUTTING DOWN ON WOODIES: Think you're safe zipped up? Think again. In February 2000, Arizona lawmaker "Carrie Nation" proposed House Bill 2360 to outlaw male genitalia appearing in strip joints "in a discernibly turgid state, even if completely and opaquely covered." This bill would make boners a crime and also criminalize all but hand-to-hand tipping at a distance of three feet. The bill, which passed through the Government Reform Committee, also sought to regulate female genitalia in a "state of sexual stimulation or arousal." Nation did not make clear how the law would be enforced.

Meanwhile, Michigan, Florida, Nebraska, Pennsylvania, and Kansas have decided that lewd conduct includes both lap dances (where the dancer rubs her groin or breasts against a man's groin and sometimes moans in alleged pleasure) and masturbation (by dancers and admirers alike). This definition was enough to shut many strip clubs down. Because of this, strippers may ask suspected cops to masturbate to prove they are not law enforcement. (However, some cops have reportedly proffered acceptable excuses and just watched.)

Strip Club Etiquette In most states, going to your standard strip joint will only leave you broke, drunk, and horny. But if some people had their way, you wouldn't even have to undress to be guilty of indecent exposure. You could just watch the girls and let nature take its course to get yourself in trouble.

If history is any guide, strip clubs will always be around in one form or another. Remember, though, that they range in service and character. If you want the least legal hassling, you can go to one that features women gyrating in bikinis. But if you want the full monty, then just assume that the place is on police watch. (You might also want to factor in that many legislatures have passed laws preventing most all-naked places from serving alcohol. A correlation between pubic hair and drunken disorderliness? Who knew?) In between these two are tassels and pasties and all sorts of other garb to keep the place running nice and legal.

> **UNDERWEAR NIGHT IN UTAH:** Blue Bar's weekly underwear night didn't go over so well with the local gentry in Salt Lake—lewd behavior abounded. Initially, the Blue Bar's liquor license was only suspended for sixty days. But, during a private party, police witnessed naked boys tending bar, sodomy (both kinds!), genital "caressing," and "actual masturbation." (It's unclear if the cops were invited guests or Peeping Toms.) State officials had heard enough. The club was shut down and its owner was fined $11,000.

A legitimate place, like Scores in New York, has the air of a gentlemen's club, and the women are on par with supermodels. They also cost a fortune. Your money ensures that well-muscled bouncers will be watching your every move. However, regardless of its reputation, any club that allows masturbation and the like is usually breaking the law (and so is the masturbator).

Porn Theaters

Unlike strip clubs, there are not many upscale porn theaters.

Street Law Concept #24: Porn Theater

Just like a regular movie theater, only it shows adult movies. Generally, the movies are at least rated X, which indicates that actual genitalia will be shown. Whether the sex on screen is mimed or real depends on the theater you're in.

This is probably because, while masturbation in most strip joints is unusual, it's more or less the point in porn theaters. Unfortunately, that doesn't make it legal. When indecent exposure statutes are not used to prosecute mooning, flashing, or peeing on the sidewalk, they can be used to bust you for exposing yourself in a public place—even if it's generally assumed (tacitly or explicitly) that you will be doing so, and even if no one is offended or alarmed by your conduct.

To illustrate our point, we present children's show host and general sex fiend Paul "Pee-wee Herman" Reubens. As we all know, Pee-wee was busted stroking himself to a showing of *Nurse Nancy* in a porn theater in 1991. Even though the theater owners expected that their customers would be gratifying themselves, Pee-wee was charged with indecent exposure during a police raid.

PEE-WEE'S ARTISTIC PLAYHOUSE: Pee-wee the Connoisseur? When Pee-wee was arrested again in November 2001 for possession of child pornography, police recovered about thirty thousand images from his photography collection and from personal computers. Authorities argued that 170 pictures involved minors engaging in sexual conduct. Pee-wee claimed that the cops "mischaracterized" his pictures as obscene, and instead claimed that his collection should be characterized as art. Some of the pictures were over a hundred years old, and some were legal at the time they were produced. Nonetheless, Pee-wee pled guilty to a misdemeanor obscenity charge, in exchange for a dismissal of the child pornography charge. He was sentenced to a $100 fine and three years' probation.

Additionally, Pee-wee won't be allowed unsupervised contact with children, and must undergo a year of counseling. After sentencing, Pee-wee still denied his collection was obscene, but claimed he wanted to avoid a "circuslike" trial.

Private Porn Booths

Since we're big advocates of privacy, you might think that we recommend a private porn booth rather than sitting in a dirty theater. But there are some rules here, too.

Street Law Concept #25: Porn Booth

A porn booth is a private booth where an individual might view a movie or, occasionally, a live stripper (or two). Porn booths may be shared, and more than one booth might be viewing the same stripper.

The video you're watching can't violate any obscenity laws, and all the actors must be over eighteen. The theater must also be in compliance with city zoning, public nuisance, and public health laws. If you've actually done all the above research, then, yes, it is legal to stand with your hands at your sides and watch a porno in a private booth in a public theater. Whip it out, and you are risking arrest. Stick it in the "glory hole," and your trouble may just be beginning.

Glory hole? you ask innocently: Ah, yes. For those of you who are pure of heart and mind, let us explain.

Street Law Concept #26: Glory Hole

Glory holes are holes cut into shared walls of porn booths or toilet stalls. Adventurous guys stick their penises through these holes in hopes of encountering a like-minded individual on the other side.

If the person sitting on the other side is a police officer, you can be busted for indecent exposure, even if the cop has signaled to you that glory waits on his side of the hole.

OLD GLORY: Texas's indecent exposure statute outlaws exposure of your private parts if you are "reckless" about exposing them to someone who might be offended. "Capone" learned about this one day while in a booth at the Allstar porn shop in Houston, Texas. When he saw someone's fingers protruding from the glory hole in an "inviting" way, Capone stuck his penis through the hole. He was promptly busted for indecent exposure by Officer "Eliot Ness." An expert on local glory holes, Officer Ness estimated that 95 percent of the time he was in a private booth (and he'd been in "thousands"), a penis appeared in the glory hole. Capone argued that since anonymous sex was normal at the Allstar, he had not been reckless when he accepted Ness's invitation. After all, who at the Allstar would have been offended? The Texas Court of Appeals disagreed. It upheld the conviction, finding that an "ordinary person" meant a non-Allstar regular, and that person would have been offended. Furthermore, Capone did not know who was on the other side.

Sex Clubs

So maybe watching isn't enough—you're more of the hands-on type. Luckily for you, sex clubs and swingers parties are coming back in style, particularly in the big city.

Street Law Concept #27: Sex/Swingers Club

A private club where various members meet to indulge in various sexual activities. Generally, all members must be over eighteen. There may be a membership fee to belong to the sex club, but no money should change hands during or dependent on the sex acts.

But even though the party or club is closed to the general public, it can still be considered a public place and you can still get arrested during a raid. As the examples below illustrate, the more established and raunchier the party, the more likely it will be busted, along with everyone inside.

POSSIBLY THE GROSSEST CASE WE'VE ENCOUNTERED: Owners of the X-rated Melody Theater—a legend in Inkster, Michigan—were charged under the state's racketeering statute with operating a "lewd criminal enterprise." According to the police, who spent over a month working "undercover" in the Melody, the theater had separate sections for anal sex, oral sex, and a middle section for "people who just really wanted to masturbate." The police finally raided the place, seizing more than five hundred videos, two hundred raunchy magazines and books, and two hundred "sex devices," and arresting fifteen people, including lawyers, teachers, and some "businessmen." Even after unlucky crews were sent to clean up the randy mess, the theater continued to test positive for semen, well, everywhere. The owners were ordered to demolish the theater within ninety days at their expense, deed the property to the city, permanently refrain from owning a similar business in those parts, and pay $1 million in fines.

Generally, the more private the place for the swinging party, the less legal trouble there is. Precautions must be taken to ensure that minors are not involved, and that money never, ever changes hands.

OBSCENITY

Obscenity is one of the most complex areas of criminal law. What is obscene on television might not be on a video. What is obscene in Oklahoma may not be in New York City. You can be charged with possessing obscene material, being obscene, or producing obscenity in a variety of circumstances. So take this chapter as nothing more than an introduction. We're just here to give you a quick rundown. If you're a porn producer or performance artist, you need more than our help.

Definitions

Okay, since we're talking about the law, "dirty" is just not good enough as a definition.

Street Law Concept #28: Obscenity

The generally accepted definition of obscenity is that when viewed as a whole, the material, publication, or object appeals to a prurient interest, describes sex in an offensive way, and lacks any serious literary, artistic, or political or scientific value.

For something to be considered obscene, the work must appeal to the "prurient" interests.

Street Law Concept #29: Prurient Interest

Something that has a shameful, morbid, or degrading interest in nudity, sex, or bodily functions—as opposed to a simply honest and curious approach to sex.

It must also depict sex in a patently offensive way (a cum shot, for example). And it must totally lack serious literary, artistic, political, or scientific value.

Street Law Concept #30: Pornography

Any publication, material, or film that depicts sexual acts in a way that appeals to prurient interests. Not all pornography is obscene.

Why isn't pornography automatically obscene? Well, for one thing, it's really, really hard to prove that something totally lacks artistic value. It's a high standard, and even *Horny Jailbait Cheerleaders* could have some artistic value. Yes, it seems ridiculous, but a lot of sex-ridden movies claim to be art films, and many art films are filled with gratuitous sex scenes. Also, deciding whether something is obscene is up to the jury, usually made up of average people. You might think that you know obscenity when you see it, but getting eleven people to agree with you is a totally different story.

Possession of Obscene Material

Generally, just owning dirty movies is not enough for an obscenity charge. (Exception: child pornography. Mere possession of this will get you busted immediately, regardless of your excuse.) However, if you bring your porn out to the public, you risk arrest. Sell your porn (or obscene devices) and you could be facing hard time, depending on what state you're in. Generally, once the porn or obscene material is out of the house, the greater the risk of the bust.

THE BIG BLACK DILDOS OF THE LONGHORN STATE: A Texas Ranger pulled over "Lady Godiva" in November 2002 for a DUI and discovered seventeen dildos in the trunk of her car. Since the law in Texas allows investigators to assume that anyone with over six "obscene items" is intending to "promote" them, Godiva was charged with promoting obscene devices. It didn't seem to matter that Godiva was a distributor for Slumber Parties Inc., a company that claims to be "where Tupperware Parties meets Victoria's Secret." The company hosts women-only parties where potential customers can view the wares, from sex toys to lotions to "private bedroom accessories." Despite her explanation, Godiva could've faced up to two years in jail. Instead, she pled guilty to the DUI so that the obscenity charge would be dropped. Godiva was sentenced to forty hours of community service and paid $276 in court costs. Not surprisingly, Godiva quit her job with Slumber Parties in exchange for less troublesome work.

Usually you have to knowingly try to sell or promote your obscene material. However, in some states (such as Illinois), you can get busted if you recklessly disregarded the possibility that the material might be obscene.

> **Street Law Concept #31: Reckless Disregard**
> When you do something with reckless disregard, you're not intentionally trying to cause trouble. But you're actively ignoring danger, acting rashly or foolishly, or seem otherwise indifferent to the consequences. An example would be shooting a gun in a crowded room without actually intending to hit anyone. If you intended to hit one particular person, then you're acting "knowingly" or with "intent."

Chart 9: Possessing Obscene Material

In most states, as we've said, merely possessing obscene material isn't enough. The court needs to find that you intended to "sell" or "promote" the material. The courts have various ways of determining this—the number of objects/materials, the packaging, the offensiveness, etc.

City	Maximum Fine	Maximum Jail Time	Other Issues
Los Angeles	$1,000	6 months	Plus $5 and/or plus 1 day in jail for every obscene object, to a maximum of $10,000 and/or 360 days in jail
District of Columbia	$1,000	6 months	If you have some equipment to "reproduce" at least 3 copies of obscene material, that's evidence of intent to promote
Miami	$1,000	1 year	NS

City	Maximum Fine	Maximum Jail Time	Other Issues
Chicago	$2,500	1 year	It's a crime if you "should have known" the material was obscene. Also, see D.C.
Las Vegas	$1,000	6 months	There will be a special proceeding to determine if something is obscene. If it is found obscene, the object/material will be destroyed
New York	$1,000	1 year	"Promoting" includes "giving" and "lending" material
Dallas	$4,000	1 year	Possession of more than 6 obscene items automatically leads to promotion charge

Cursing

You may not believe it, but, yes—simple cursing can get you in trouble. While, of course, it depends on the circumstances, the good news is that merely uttering a bad word or displaying an obscenity is not enough to be charged with obscenity. In certain situations, though, it can get you busted for disorderly conduct.

TEXAS TAKES ANOTHER SCALP: In New Braunfels, Texas, eighteen-year-old Marilyn Manson fan "Billy Budd" got a quick and dirty lesson on the First Amendment,

Texas style. Somehow, his I AM THE GOD OF FUCK Manson T-shirt had offended some fellow shoppers, who promptly notified the police. The cop took Budd outside and decided to take a poll, asking passersby whether they found the shirt offensive. Some did, some didn't, but Budd was arrested anyway for a "lewd display" and disorderly conduct. He spent three hours in jail before posting bond. The Texas ACLU took up the case, which was ultimately dismissed on technical grounds.

Curse words vary from state to state, neighborhood to neighborhood. After all, it's hard to be offended if you don't know that you're being insulted. But some words, too universally indelicate to be mentioned here, are always red flags to the government. The more prominently you display these words, the more attention you're going to get from the authorities.

SODOMY: NOW GOVERNMENT APPROVED?

After many decades of being considered "deviant sexual intercourse," the Supreme Court has found sodomy to be legal.

Street Law Concept #32: Sodomy

Originally considered a crime against nature like bestiality, sodomy is now generally defined as oral or anal sex. Sodomy might be consensual or forced (which is still a crime) and can take place between homosexuals, heterosexuals, or anyone in between.

Originally, in 1986, the Supreme Court decreed in

Bowers v. Hardwick that there was, alas, no fundamental right to a blow job. After the Hardwick decision, states continued to enforce these ancient, yet formidable sodomy laws with varying degrees of enthusiasm.

> **A BRIEF HISTORY OF HARDWICK:** Twenty-eight-year-old bar-tender Michael Hardwick was home enjoying "mutual fellatio" (aka 69ing) with his (male) guest, when the police came to his house to serve a warrant for unpaid parking tickets. Hardwick's roommate let the cops in and directed them to Hardwick's bedroom. When the cops witnessed what was going on, they arrested both men for violating Georgia's sodomy law. "J. Edgar Hoover," Georgia's attorney general at the time, defended the sodomy statute in the Supreme Court, arguing that ancient scholars considered even consensual sodomy a crime as odious as rape. Hoover and the ancient scholars won, and sodomy laws were upheld. (Incidentally, Hoover was forced to acknowledge a fifteen-year affair when he ran for governor a couple years later. His mistress was quoted at the time as saying, "As far as sodomy is concerned, [J. Edgar Hoover] is a hypocrite.")

Up until recently, sodomy charges were often used to target gay men and lesbians. For example, the State of Virginia recently used sodomy laws to deprive Sharon Bottoms custody of her adopted child. A Virginia court ruled that she was unfit as a parent, in part due to the "felonious sexual conduct inherent in lesbianism." In other words, since Bottoms, as a lesbian, committed a felony every time she had sex, she was a criminal and an unfit parent.

But a new day has dawned. In a recent landmark decision, the Supreme Court has decreed that all sodomy laws—whether they punish heterosexual or homosexual sodomy, or both—are illegal.

SODOMY LAW UPDATE: More than a decade after Hardwick was jailed for a blow job, police in Texas stumbled on another sodomy in progress. Responding to a false report of an armed man at an apartment complex, police found "Achilles" Lawrence and "Patroclus" Garner engaging in "homosexual conduct." The crime fighters seized the couple, who ultimately pleaded no contest to violating Texas's "homosexual conduct law" and paid a $200 fine. (The man who directed the police to the couple's apartment was convicted of filing a false report.) The Supreme Court, in a historic 6–3 decision, ruled that Americans were entitled to some "sexual privacy," and that the sodomy laws of Texas—as well as all other states—were unconstitutional.

Since the Supreme Court's decision in *Lawrence v. Texas,* politicians have become sharply divided. Some, like conservative Supreme Court justice Antonin Scalia, moan about the fall of American values and the rise of the "homosexual agenda." Others have seen this as a new era for gay rights and sexual freedom. Next step? The legalization of gay marriage. While states such as Hawaii and Vermont have allowed certain same-sex civil unions, gay activists rightly claim that these unions don't have the same rights and benefits of heterosexual marriage. In some states, gay activists and sympathetic politicians are finding the right to marriage in the equal protection clauses of state constitutions. While *Lawrence* wasn't directly responsible for each state controversy, the case seems to have inspired more gay couples to fight for their right to marry.

SOLICITATION: WERE YOU ASKING FOR IT?

There's nothing sexier than a dirty little whisper from your date in a movie theater. But while dirty talk can be the ultimate safe sex, talking about how much you would like a blow job can get you into as much trouble as getting a blow job, particularly if you are talking to a cop.

Street Law Concept #33: Criminal Solicitation

Solicitation occurs when you request, command, or encourage someone to commit a crime or attempt to commit a crime. When you solicit a crime and get caught, you'll be charged with the crime that you were soliciting the other person for.

BUSTED FOR TALKING DIRTY: Before the *Lawrence* decision, "Othello" of Topeka, Kansas, was sitting in his car one afternoon in Gage Park, known as a gay cruising joint. He was approached by "Iago" (an undercover cop), who asked if he was "a friend" and whether he was "into that." Othello, thinking his afternoon was looking up, said that he was a friend. Iago asked him what he liked to do, and Othello told the cop that he did not like anal sex, but "admitted" that he liked blow jobs. Asked by the cop if he would "do that to me," Othello, assuming they would go to his place, said, "Yeah, sure," and was promptly busted for solicitation of sodomy. The Kansas Supreme Court liked his conviction so much they unanimously affirmed it.

Criminal solicitation can occur whether you actually ask or if you let your body do the talking. If you're waving your "turgid genitalia" (boner) at an undercover cop in a public john, as pop star George "I Want Your Sex" Michael was busted doing, courts will infer that you were inviting the cop to partake in a bit of sodomy, even though you haven't actually asked.

GEORGE MICHAEL SUED BY BEVERLY HILLS COP: Michael was busted for committing a "lewd act," but the police would only say that he was alone, he was doing something, and the cop watched him do it. Michael on the other hand blamed the incident on his inability to "turn down a free meal" and was quoted as saying that when "someone is waving their genitalia at you, you don't automatically assume they're an officer of the law." Not amused, "Captain Ahab," the cop who observed Michael getting lewd with his bad self, has sued him for slander. Ahab is complaining that Michael has publicly accused him of entrapment and mocked him, particularly in the video "Outside," which parodies the incident. Unfortunately for Ahab, the case eventually got thrown out by the court.

PIMPING AND HOING: PROSTITUTION LAW

Once, picking up a prostitute meant driving around deserted streets looking for seedy, drugged-out women (or men). Now, high-class escort services are available through your phone and the Internet. You can get a classy, attractive, sometimes even educated companion who probably even takes credit cards. Where's the harm?

It all depends on whom you talk to. Many people feel

that prostitution is a "victimless" crime—after all, everyone involved is a consenting adult. Some demand that prostitution either be decriminalized (just repealing the laws that make prostitution illegal) or legalized (making prostitution a legal, organized, and regulated industry). Their argument? "It's sex and the free market. Which one are you against?"

Whatever happens in the future, prostitution is at least a misdemeanor in every state except for Nevada (more on Nevada later). Some states will even publish the names of johns in newspapers.

The first thing you need to know is this: no matter what your background, anyone can be a prostitute or a john. Just because you're not picking up the so-called ladies on the street corner in the warehouse district doesn't mean you're safe from arrest. And just because you've only had paid sex with "good friends" doesn't make you any less of a prostitute.

Furthermore, whatever stigma society assigns to prostitution, the penalties for prostitutes and their johns are virtually the same. That's right. It doesn't matter who was getting paid—if you offered to exchange sex for money, or vice versa, then you're getting similar penalties whether you're getting paid or doing the paying.

PLAYING WITHOUT PAYING: Officer "Rochester" of the Seattle police department was on patrol last September when he was flagged down by "Jane," a prostitute. Jane told him that she was having a problem with a john who refused to pay for the blow job she had just administered. Rochester, not quite believing what he was hearing, asked the wronged service provider what she wanted him to do about it. Jane felt it was Rochester's duty as public servant to see that she was paid. Unmoved, Rochester arrested both the prostitute and the cheap bastard.

On the other hand, cracking down on prostitution is often not a court's top crime-fighting priority. In most cases you'll pay well below the maximum fine, get community service, or even just probation. It's unlikely that you'll spend much if any time in jail, whether you're a prostitute or the customer. Still, some things could get you in serious trouble, like being a repeat offender. Suddenly judges aren't yawning when they look at your rap sheet, and your string of misdemeanors could lead to a felony conviction.

So whether you're picking up drag queens in a sex club or calling up an escort service for your bachelor party, or paying an ex for a quickie—in the end, it's all the same thing.

Defining Sex

Despite what certain ex-presidents would have you believe, virtually any sexual conduct or contact is considered sex in the eyes of the law. (This includes presidential blow jobs and Clinton's famous cigar trick.)

Street Law Concept #34: Fornication/Sex

In addition to normal intercourse, most states also define sex as fondling of the genitals, the anus, or any part of the female breast. Spanking and S&M can also be considered sex. Fornication is sex between two people not married to each other.

Watching: Not Exactly Sex?

In most states, the crime of prostitution does not require the john to actually have sex with the prostitute. So long as you pay someone to have sex with you or with herself or with a friend(s), you have solicited prostitution. It doesn't matter if you play with yourself or not.

And just so you know, it might be worse for you if you try to pay someone to make out with her friend. In Texas, for example, soliciting another to engage in sex for a fee can cost you up to $4,000 or one year in jail. Simply sleeping with a prostitute gets you less. It depends on how the law is interpreted.

> **POLE DANCING UNDER THE LAW:** The "Inferno" Club had been on the police radar for some time, and Officer "Dante" was sent undercover to see how far those ladies would really go. The owner of the Inferno, "Beatrice," also did some dancing herself and was busted for pimping, pandering, and prostitution. On appeal, Beatrice argued that the prosecution improperly informed the jury that "skin-on-skin" contact wasn't necessary to establish a sex act. The appeals court disagreed and noted that even when sexual gratification occurred through a thin layer of cloth, it was still sex.

Nonmonetary Compensation

Think you can get around prostitution laws with the old barter system? Think again. Prostitution does not require actual money to change hands. If you exchange anything of monetary value for sex, you risk arrest. For example, the New York statute makes it clear that prostitution is the exchange of sex for money *or other consideration*.

> **Street Law Concept #35: Consideration**
> The definition of *consideration* is complicated, but generally, it means something of value (a good or a service) intentionally exchanged for something else of value (a good or a service). A gift, therefore, cannot be viewed as consideration, as you usually give it without asking for anything in return.

In the State of New York, therefore, if you promise to exchange your DVD player for a roll in the hay, you're soliciting prostitution. "Value" includes services as well, so offering to wash someone's car for a blow job is, once again, prostitution. Moral? Sex can only be exchanged for sex. Whatever type of sex you decide is fair exchange is entirely up to you and your partner(s).

Now we know what you're thinking: this could get tricky. What about all those times that guys buy their dates really expensive dinners, in hopes of getting laid? Are they soliciting prostitution? What about the ladies (or men) who seem to demand expensive gifts before giving it up? Are they hookers?

It can be a fine line, but the key in the above situations is that the exchange is implicit—nobody is overtly saying they'll trade sex for money or vice versa. It's fine to lavish your "girlfriend" with gaudy jewelry and vacations (or business trips), but sex for money is sex for money. You might have an unspoken agreement. But if you ever verbalize it, or if your lady (or dude) starts asking for the jewels up front, consider trading her (or him) in for a less demanding model.

The Spouse Exception

If your spouse has decided to charge for sex, you might be free and clear of a prostitution charge. It depends on the state. Florida, for example, makes it clear in the prostitution statute that the people involved must not be married to one another. If they are, then they can exchange sex for just about anything they want, including money. It's the same in California. But remember, it depends on the wording of the particular statute. In the District of Columbia, for example, there's no language saying that the prostitute and the john must not be married to each other. And if the statute doesn't make it clear that prostitution can only occur between an unmarried couple (or, at least, not married to each other), then some overzealous DA can still charge you (though, in most cases, the judge will probably laugh it out of court).

Welcome to Nevada

Just the thought of Nevada makes some people drool. Legalized prostitution! Not just that, but nice, clean brothels with beds and beautiful women and a bar downstairs. But before you get excited, you might want to know that prostitution is *not* legal in the entire state of Nevada. For one thing, if you have any fantasies of staying at the Luxor with a fabulous and legal call girl, think again. It isn't legal in Las Vegas. It isn't legal in Reno, Carson City, or Lake Tahoe either, because state law forbids legalized prostitution in heavily populated areas. If you're looking for a house of ill-repute, then strap on your spurs, cowboy. You're going to the country.

Even in areas where prostitution is legal, you'll have to go to a brothel—it's illegal to solicit from the street.

And while it may be public knowledge where the "cathouses" (as they're so elegantly called) are, you won't find any advertisements—advertising prostitution is illegal. Which makes it hard to know which counties have legalized prostitution and which haven't (there are still city ordinances against it in some areas). Get caught in the wrong area and you're facing a prostitution or solicitation charge just as you would in any other state. The chart below shows that the fine for soliciting in a county that doesn't have legalized prostitution can be just as steep—if not more steep—than in other states.

However, if you do prove resourceful enough to get the numbers of some brothels, then enjoy. One thing you might want to remember, though: wear a condom. That's not a judgment on the ladies—it's just that it's the law in Nevada that all brothel clients wear a condom.

Another thing: show up drunk and you're probably going to pay extra.

Pandering and Juveniles
Heidi Fleiss named her memoir *Pandering*. It sounds dirty, but what is it?

Street Law Concept #36: Pandering
Essentially the same as pimping, pandering also includes convincing someone to be a prostitute or promoting obscene materials.

We associate pimps with guys in fancy hats, gold chains, and platform shoes, but if you get a hooker for your friend's bachelor party, and it somehow goes horribly wrong, then you could be faced with a pandering charge.

Pandering is a felony, which means *at least* one year in prison.

> **FREE JACK:** In 1998, police were called to a house in Santa Barbara, California, to the scene of an assault and robbery. What they discovered was "Jill's Touch Massage," where Jill and her associates performed sensual massage services . . . and sometimes more. Naturally, the police charged Jill with prostitution and pandering . . . but also charged her husband, "Jack." Jack had no part in the business and claimed to know nothing about what went on behind closed doors. However, a portion of Jack and Jill's bills were paid from the massage business, and they shared the house and the joint account. Jill fled and is still on the lam, but Jack was found guilty of pimping and "keeping a house of ill-fame." The original money-laundering charge (because of the joint accounts) was eventually dropped.

You should also look out for those girls/boys/etc. who look too young to be true. If they are, then you're in deep trouble. Under eighteen is one thing—you'll usually have to pay a hefty fine, at least. Under 16—or less—is a whole different story. You could be looking at a statutory rape charge, which is a felony.

Street Law Concept #37: Statutory Rape

Statutory rape occurs when you have sex with someone who, because of her/his age, is not legally capable of consenting to sex (i.e., isn't old enough to know how to consent). The age varies from state to state, but usually ranges from eleven to eighteen. Your age also matters.

To be charged with statutory rape, you don't have to know the girl was underage. She could've lied to you, shown you a fake ID, whatever. The mere fact that she is underage, and you had sex with her, makes you guilty. However, your age matters as well—if you're also under eighteen (or in some cases under twenty-one) then the penalties differ in certain states.

HOT FOR TEACHER?: The statutory rape charge can go either way. In 1997, thirty-five-year-old elementary-school teacher "Bonnie" was pregnant . . . but not by her husband. The father of the baby was a thirteen-year-old student, later identified as "Clyde." Bonnie—who already had three children—was convicted of statutory rape and sentenced to six months in jail. Though she appeared remorseful and contrite at her hearing, Bonnie continued her affair with Clyde and was re-arrested. She was also pregnant again, but was nonetheless sentenced to seven years in prison. Both her children by Clyde were placed in custody of Clyde's mother. Bonnie and Clyde still claim to be deeply in love with each other.

And speaking of the young at heart, if you're the old-fashioned type who still likes to pick up girls on the street corner, make sure you know your neighborhood. In Illinois, if you're within a thousand feet of a school, you're guilty of a felony.

A simple prostitution or solicitation charge might result in a slap on the wrist. Two might be a heavier fine or jail time . . . or a low-level felony.

Chart 10: Prostitution/Solicitation of Prostitution

Remember: You can be charged with solicitation of prostitution or even prostitution just by asking someone to have sex with you for money, or making that offer. You don't actually have to have sex—or even start!

City	Maximum Fine	Jail Time	Other Issues
Los Angeles	$1,000	6 months	$70 added to fine at discretion of judge. Spouse exception
District of Columbia	$500	1–90 days	Or community service. No spouse exception listed
Miami	$500	2 months	Spouse exception
Chicago	$1,000	1 year	Spouse exception—in some cases
Las Vegas	$1,000	6 months	No spouse exception listed
New York	$500	3 months	No spouse exception listed
Dallas	$2,000	6 months	Get arrested 3 times and you have mandatory jail time. No spouse exception listed

CONCLUSION

No matter what you're into, the law is ready to have a say in your sex life. Whether you're saving yourself for marriage or have already forgotten the name of your last conquest, it's a good idea to keep your common sense— even in the heat of passion. Like most pleasures in life, sex comes in infinite varieties and everyone has his or her own special favorite. But if you find yourself being pulled in front of a judge more than once, you might want to rethink your technique. Being labeled a sex offender or charged with indecency will follow you around for a while.

CHAPTER 3

Out on the Streets: Public Misdemeanors

INTRODUCTION

A whole host of other misdemeanors can get you into trouble. And they have nothing to do with smoking, snorting, stripping, or snuggling.

This chapter covers miscellaneous misdemeanors and the laws you're breaking without even knowing it—with one caveat: there are approximately 1,287 ways to get busted that aren't covered in here. (Go ahead, check that figure.) So why keep reading? Because the listed crimes are the most common troubles of the average citizen, and the most common busts by neighborhood police. The odds of you being busted for disturbing the nest of the rare Booshu bird are pretty slim. The odds of you getting busted for disorderly conduct, however, are pretty high (disorderly conduct is a favorite among law enforcement officials). Can these miscellaneous misdemeanors get you into any real trouble? Of course. But as a small-time offender, you're only really concerned with a handful of applicable state laws. There are always city ordinances, but ordinances and violations are pretty minor—show up in court or pay a fine or get off with a warning. This chapter covers the middle ground: somewhere between littering and armed robbery.

DISORDERLY CONDUCT

Disorderly conduct doesn't sound like much trouble. It's a slap on the wrist, right? Well, maybe. But it's also the broadest charge a cop can bring against you. It's everywhere, it covers everything, and you don't even have to be trying to be disorderly. It's a legal catchall: whatever you think you're getting away with, a cop can try to bust you for disorderly conduct.

Street Law Concept #38: Disorderly Conduct

While definitions vary, disorderly conduct includes any conduct where you intentionally deprive the community (or a group of citizens) of peace, quiet, or normal enjoyment of public property. It's also known as disturbing the peace.

You might wonder what the boundaries of disorderly conduct are. A basic look at various statutes uncovers the following five types of disorderly conduct: ruckus, indecent disorderly conduct, obstruction, dangerous situation, and annoying of public officials.

Before you go on, remember that even if you think you're not being disorderly, you can still be charged for disorderly conduct. The best way to tell is whether a cop is warning you to leave a situation. Ignoring him will result in a disorderly conduct charge. However, not all states require cops to issue a warning before arresting you.

Ruckus

Ruckus is by far the most common version of disorderly conduct. There are two basic kinds to think about.

The fighting ruckus occurs when you start a fight or do something that would get someone to start a fight with you. This includes shouting curse words at someone from across the street, getting into someone's face, goading someone on, or backing your friends when they get unruly. It does not matter if you started the fight or are just defending yourself. It does not matter if you didn't think the other guy would take your insults seriously enough to start a fight. All it takes is a loud, angry voice, some threatening or obscene gestures, and a public place. Now, really fighting can get you in trouble, and there's more on that later. For a disorderly conduct charge to occur, it means the cops couldn't bust you on assault. So the fighting described in this section is just people yelling and threatening to knock each other out.

LOOK OUT, KING KONG!: Weddings can be crazy, but sometimes the worst part is . . . the bride? "Florence Nightingale," of North Haven, Connecticut, was so enraged that the bar closed after her reception that she began yelling and cursing, throwing everything from the wedding cake to the gifts. (Hope nothing was fragile, sweetheart.) Florence was spotted storming down the street in her wedding gown, but when cops tried to pick her up, she resisted, cursed, tried to bite a cop, and threw her wedding ring to the ground. "Bridezilla," as she was dubbed by the press, was ordered to pay a $90 fine and seek substance-abuse and anger-management counseling.

The noisy ruckus is quite similar to the fighting ruckus, except you don't need another party. You're just making a racket, either by yelling or by knocking garbage cans around or by shouting about what a bastard your ex-boyfriend is.

This can include times when you're blasting your stereo, although that can be nuisance as well. Yelling into your cell phone can get you in trouble, too, so save the dramatic confrontations for your home. The noisy ruckus is usually the province of the Drunken Doofus or the Frat Boy Pledge, but, occasionally, sober folks have been known to take it to the streets as well.

But wait—what about the First Amendment? The Bill of Rights? Why can't I shout my opinions at the top of my lungs if I'm feeling patriotic? Well, to bust you for a ruckus charge (especially a fighting ruckus charge), the cops don't have to worry about your First Amendment rights if it seemed that you were likely to use violence or there was a threat of violence. "Fighting words" are not protected by the First Amendment.

Street Law Concept #39: Fighting Words

These are words that are so inflammatory and so aggressive that they are likely to incite violence in a public place. The Supreme Court has stated that these words are not relevant to the "exposition of ideas." Meaning? They don't contribute anything useful— you're not actually saying anything that needs to be protected.

Your First Amendment rights are usually on hold if you look like you're going to start a fight or engage in any behavior that could incite others to fight.

HIS MOTHER DOESN'T COUNT, EITHER: "Sigmund Freud" was distraught, shouting and refusing to accept the restraining order the cop was trying to give him. He even put his hands behind his back and bumped the cop with his body. Freud was promptly arrested for assaulting a cop, and for disorderly conduct. However, the disorderly conduct charge was thrown out because the disturbance occurred on Freud's mother's driveway. For a disorderly conduct charge to hold up in Massachusetts, the conduct has to be in a public area, or likely to affect the public at large. The court in this case found that all the action took place on private land, and no one but Freud's mother and the cops were around. The cops themselves couldn't be considered "the public at large." Lucky Freud: the jury found him not guilty of the assault charge, too.

Indecent Disorderly Conduct

If the cops can't bust you for lewd conduct (because you weren't trying to shock or offend), they can bust you for disorderly conduct. This includes instances when you're naked but not having sex (streaking, for example). You might think that pretty girls can do whatever they want, but think about this: for every hot college girl who gets naked, there's a grumpy old lady who'll call the cops.

Obscene gestures can get you busted as well, but they usually have to be repeated and really obscene. Generally it has to be more than words, unless you're shouting and indicating that you're about to start a fight. The middle finger to another driver on the road may not do it, but if you're shouting and flipping off the president of the United States in your underwear, then you're really working toward a disorderly conduct charge.

And you should know that if you enter upon some girl's property to watch her take a shower, you're asking for trouble (at the least a disorderly conduct charge, with a trespass charge thrown in for good measure).

Obstruction

Even if you're the quiet type, and fully clothed, you can be busted for disorderly conduct. Say, for example, you're in a protest or demonstration. Or, you decide that you want to have a Me Day Parade—only you don't have a parade permit. Even if you and your friends are peaceably milling around on a sidewalk, if you're slowing down traffic (even pedestrian traffic) or refusing to move after you've been warned, you can be charged with disorderly conduct.

Street Law Concept #40: The Right to Assembly

The right of assembly comes from the Constitution. You are entitled to gather in public to air your opinions or grievances or petition for change. The assembly must be peaceful—not violent or dangerous. Picketing your job or for change is protected by the right of assembly.

Say you're by yourself. Don't worry, you can still cause trouble. For example, say you're trying to save a parking space for your friend who's circling the block. If another car is trying to park there (and it's a public place), your refusing to move can be construed as disorderly conduct. The activity seems harmless enough, but a cop in a bad mood might spot you as a troublemaker. Ditto for situations where you take the law into your own hands. You think the school grounds should be locked after seven so drug dealers can't congregate there. Buy your own lock, chain up the gates, and a disorderly conduct charge could soon follow.

Generally, the guidelines are that your behavior had no legitimate, legal purpose. You might think that saving a parking space in this day and age is an act of ultimate responsibility, but the guy trying to park the car probably won't agree.

Dangerous Situation

Any of the above could create a dangerous situation. However, so could pulling out a gun in a public place. Sure, the gun could be unloaded, you could have a permit—it may even be a toy gun. But in some states and in certain situations, this could lead to a disorderly conduct charge. (If you're lucky. And more than one cop has shot at a supposedly armed individual who was just taking out his wallet.) Imagine that you're sitting in the next booth to someone who does that in a diner—it could start a stampede.

Other ways of creating a dangerous situation? Pulling the fire alarm at work. Scaring the bus driver while he tries to make his stops. Ill-advised practical jokes, like cherry bombs. A lot of "harmless" pranks can cause a lot of trouble for people—like yelling "bomb" in a movie theater. (Actually, that could get you busted for a lot worse. In this day and age, a disorderly conduct charge is a relatively minor punishment for that.) Most states also prohibit wearing masks on any day other than Halloween.

As in the case of obstruction, the law must prove that your behavior that created the dangerous situation did not serve any legitimate purpose other than being a pain in the ass. Protest, therefore, can be considered a legitimate purpose.

LOVE CAN BE BLIND . . . AND DUMB. REALLY DUMB: "Lady Chatterley" was so in love with her boyfriend she couldn't bear to be parted from him—not even if her parents took her on a ten-day cruise to Hawaii. So eager was our young lover to return to her man that she devised a way to turn the boat around . . . by sending bomb threats against the twenty-four hundred passengers and crew. This brilliant scheme failed on multiple levels. First, the ship docked in Hawaii anyway, to be extensively searched for weapons and bombs. Second, after Chatterley confessed, a federal court judge sentenced her to *two years* in federal prison. That's 730 days because she couldn't wait 10 days. Was he worth it? Who knows?

Annoying of Public Officials

Many states will charge you for disorderly conduct if you submit a false report to public officials—not just the police and fire departments, but with the Board of Health, Department of Children's Services, etc. So if you think you're going to get even with your ex-wife and report that she's abusive to your kids, think again. If it's proven that you knew the report was false, you'll be busted—either for filing a false report or disorderly conduct.

And of course, it's generally a bad idea to report fake crimes or imaginary fires to the authorities. Even as a gag. No one but you will think it's funny.

The above guidelines of disorderly conduct are just that—guidelines. City ordinances can include charges of trespass, vandalism, obscenity, public drunkenness, etc., in a disorderly conduct charge. If you're lucky, that is. If not, you could be charged with disorderly conduct and one of the following other public misdemeanors.

Chart 11: Charges of Disorderly Conduct

Remember, disorderly conduct is a legal catchall, and therefore one of the more important sections of law. If you were brawling, but not enough for an assault charge, they'll give you disorderly conduct. If you were naked, but not lewd, the disorderly conduct charge strikes again. Most protest violations will get you a disorderly conduct charge as well. If the cops arrest you for going a step further (i.e., starting a riot), then add about six months to your jail time. Ditto if you disturb a house of worship, or school.

CITY	MAXIMUM FINE	MAXIMUM JAIL TIME
Los Angeles	$1,000	6 months
District of Columbia	$250	3 months
Miami	$500	2 months
Chicago	$1,500	1 month
Las Vegas	$1,000	6 months
New York	$500	3 months
Dallas	$500	Not specified

DEMONSTRATIONS AND PROTEST

Protesters are a unique bunch, as they are one of the few groups of people who sometimes actually want to get arrested.

Your Right to Protest

The First Amendment guarantees you the right to peaceful

assembly, and by extension, protest. Whether you're in a group of thousands marching down the street, or you're just one guy waving a sign in front of a fur store, you have the right to protest against public and private practices that you think are unfair.

You aren't, however, free from the possibility of arrest. Exercising your right to protest is a system of checks and balances: you can go too far and land in jail. Here are the three elements of a successful protest.

1. Strategy

Are you a firebrand, a hothead? Do you want nothing more than to wade headlong into the good fight, start an uprising, fire up a revolution? Then protest is not for you. Most protests, no matter how large or how small, are well thought out in advance. There are exceptions, and if you see something that needs your immediate attention, you can drop everything and start marching immediately. But this is a rarity; most successful protests are organized, communal activities with specific guidelines and goals.

The first item on every agenda is the permit.

Street Law Concept #41: Permits

For certain activities involving public spaces, a permit is necessary. They are usually granted by the police and, in the case of protests, protect your right to peaceful assembly in designated areas, for a designated time.

While it's easy to be suspicious of the police giving you permits, the truth is that most permit denials occur for practical reasons: there's a parade on that street that day, or that street is closed off for construction. This is not to say that permits are not denied for political reasons; if the chief of police is getting a lot of heat for the very subject you're protesting, then your permit can be denied.

If your permit is denied, you can still plan the protest for that day. This type of protest is known as civil disobedience, used by Martin Luther King Jr. and Gandhi.

Street Law Concept #42: Civil Disobedience

This is a planned, reasonable method of protest where the protesters, as a whole, violate the boundaries and rules (if any) set down by the government for their protest.

Civil disobedience—which also includes instances where you've been given a permit, but stray outside the area the permit covers—is much more likely to get you arrested. If that isn't your goal, try to work with the police and see if you can move your protest to a different time, day, or place.

EVEN THE BIG SHOTS GET ARRESTED SOMETIMES: Jesse Jackson was one of thirteen people arrested on Labor Day, 2003, for leading a protest of more than a thousand people in support of the striking Yale University clerical workers' union. Why were these thirteen singled out? Because they intentionally blocked traffic, moving from a legal protest to civil disobedience. It's unlikely that this was accidental—certainly the reverend's arrest made national headlines, putting more heat on the negotiations.

Once you've decided on the protest, you need to gather support. How you do this is up to you; many protests are poorly publicized, while others garner national attention. Many prominent protesters have a legal team on notice about the protest and have people videotaping the protest in case it gets out of hand.

2. Synchronicity

Synchronization is not just for swimmers. You might be moved to tears when you think of the cause you're marching for, but a protest is not the time to lose your head and start surprising your fellow protesters. Whether there are a dozen protesters or thousands, and whether you're an organizer or just a participant, the key to a good protest is bringing together lots of people for a common goal. In other words, this is not the time to try to show off or grab the spotlight.

Synchronicity begins at the planning stage. The protest leaders and organizers should have a clear agenda of what they want to happen in the protest. Do you want to be on the news? Do you want to stay there all day? Is part of the point to actually block traffic? Will there be civil disobedience as a symbolic gesture? Once the agenda is mapped out, the protesters will have a better idea of what actions they're meant to take, and what they can expect.

At the protest, there should be organizers who make sure that the protesters are keeping to the agenda. This includes leading chants, passing out flyers, and making sure that protesters stay in the given physical boundaries. Go against the agenda and you're undermining the protest and the intentions of everyone else there.

The group's agenda might include getting arrested. In this case, the arrestees should still be completely in tune with the group plan. Protesters are often jailed together (so they don't "corrupt" the other prisoners.) You can continue your protest all the way to jail, but your best bet is safety in numbers, and sticking to the established game plan.

> **JUSTICE—NOT BLIND ENOUGH:** Imagine if every day you went to work, you have to pass a mass of screaming protesters, calling you names and blocking your way. Sounds like a job for the cops, right? Unfortunately, the cops, the local judge, and even the DA have made it abundantly clear they're not going to help you. Why? Because you work for Long Island Gynecological Services (LIGS), a center that performs abortions, and the Nassau district attorney is pro-life. Not only does he refuse to prosecute trespassers, but the cops are banned from arresting them in the first place. The protesters are apparently exempt from laws that govern the rest of us simply because of their religious beliefs. LIGS finally got an injunction banning them from the property.

3. Safety

Even if you're planning on getting arrested, you want to stay safe. This can be difficult if you're facedown on the pavement with a cop slamming the cuffs on you. However, there's getting arrested and then there's getting into serious trouble with the police. It is possible to do one without the other. Most of this is covered in chapter 5; however, some elements specific to protest situations are important to remember.

First of all, you might get arrested even if it's not your plan. Things may get out of hand, or the cops might just (ahem) jump the gun. You can protest your arrest, but not by standing around and arguing. One of the popular protest methods is to go limp; let your body go completely slack so the cops have to drag you away. This is a good way to protest your arrest, but remember the following: (1) cops can drop you, so use your neck muscles to keep your head up; (2) wear long sleeves and long pants to protect bare skin dragging against the sidewalk. Ouch!

Even if you're protesting against the police, never taunt or harass the cops who are actually monitoring your protest. They're facing off against a whole crowd of angry people, a situation that might make anyone tense. Don't give them any reason to use force.

Whatever your protest strategy, it should continue into jail. Some people go on a hunger strike or even go naked (which takes a lot of nerve). Police do not like to deal with protesters; it's bad public relations and the media are watching their every move. But just remember—one person on a hunger strike is at best a difficult situation, but a dozen is a publicity nightmare. Don't go off the agenda; stick to the group plan and see it through to the end.

DON'T PISS OFF THE SECRET SERVICE: "Raskolnikov" had been a political protester since the late 1960s. In 2002, he was all set to protest the government's stance in the Middle East when President George W. Bush arrived in Columbia, South Carolina, in 2002. However, the Secret Service told Raskolnikov and other protesters that they were not allowed in the restricted area. Coincidentally, the signs of Republican candidates were allowed in the restricted area. A fiery Rasky refused to leave, arguing that the Secret Service was messing with his First Amendment rights to free speech, since they allowed supporters of the president to be much closer than protesters. The judge disagreed, and Rasky was fined $500.

Protest is like anything else. The more risks you take, the more trouble you can get into. Heckling and other loud behavior can get you a nuisance charge. Streaking can get you busted for disorderly conduct or, in some cases, even indecent exposure. Throwing paint (as some antifur protesters do) can result in destruction-of-property charges, or even assault if you hit a person. How far you want to go is up to you and your demonstrating brethren. But remember this: the First Amendment wasn't created to be a Get out of Jail Free card for any and all your crazy schemes.

TRESPASS

Trespass, like disorderly conduct and nuisance, is a large and messy area of law.

Street Law Concept #43: Criminal Trespass

This crime occurs when you "wrongfully interfere" with someone else's property. The property in question is usually land or a house, and the trespasser, by definition, does not have the permission of the property's owner. You can also trespass on public property.

You can trespass in obvious ways, like walking on someone else's property. You can trespass by misusing your neighbor's garden rake—even if you return it. You can trespass by dumping junk into your neighbor's yard. You can even trespass when on public property. And no, you don't have to intend to be trespassing. Just being in the wrong place at the wrong time can get you busted.

> **BIG BROTHER ON YOUR KEYBOARD**: Trespass means going where you're not supposed to, right? Some people want it to mean more than that. The all-seeing Intel Corporation accused a fired employee, "Odysseus," of trespass because he spammed thirty-five thousand of his former colleagues in two years. Intel tried to base its claim on a California law that prohibits someone from misusing another's property even if he isn't stealing it. Their argument, theoretically, was that Intel had a right to exclude Odysseus from its Internet system (its property). If this sounds fishy to you, the California Supreme Court agreed, mostly because Intel couldn't prove that they had been injured in any way.

However, trespass law, while confusing and scary, is easier to figure out in the city than in the country. In the country, there are all those wide-open spaces, those lakes begging for fishing boats and those forests crying out for hunters. Just asking for trouble, really. In many states, landowners are no longer required to fence in their property or have many Private Property signs. If you're found fishing in someone else's lake, then you can be considered a trespasser, whether you saw a sign or not. The best defense is to somehow prove that you had permission to be on that property from its owner.

In the city, it's a bit easier to tell if you're trespassing. For example, if you have to jimmy a lock to get anywhere, you're trespassing. If you have to scale a fence, you're trespassing. And no, there does not always have to be a sign.

Street Law Concept #44: Breaking and Entering

Breaking is when you break open an enclosed space, usually by force or violence. Enclosed space usually just means some kind of building. Entering means that you or some part of you entered into that enclosed space, and not by accident. This crime is often lumped together with trespass, though with trespass, you can just wander into the wrong place. Breaking and entering is more planned, and more intentional.

What about those annoying salespeople going door-to-door? Generally, for a homeowner or shopkeeper to prosecute you for trespass, he has to specifically prohibit you from his property. A No Soliciting sign should suffice in this regard. If you see one and decide to try to sell your set of encyclopedias anyway, you're doing so at your own risk. Once they verbally warn you, don't dawdle—move fast off the property before they can call the cops.

Trespass law merges with nuisance law in some cases. If you manage to destroy someone's property without setting foot on it, you could be charged with trespass. This includes dumping sewage into someone's backyard or letting your dog repeatedly defecate on someone's stoop. Now, admittedly, this sort of thing is usually covered by nuisance law, but an enterprising officer could charge you with both.

In case you haven't figured it out, trespass doesn't just mean you physically cross a line. It includes your dog, your car, and the rock you throw at someone's window. For those of you with a green thumb, you need to be aware of the plants and trees you're planting near your property boundaries. The trees may be yours, but, in most states, your neighbor has the right to cut off any branches that fall over the property line. You're also responsible for the damage done to your neighbor's property if the tree should fall in a storm.

Public Property

All of the above examples have been for private property. It's quite possible to be banned from public property as well. For example, if the local park or dog walk closes after sunset, you could be found guilty of trespassing even if there's no gate around the park. Admittedly, the cop would have to be a real hard-ass to bust you for this, but it all depends on what you're doing on the property. (Note: bringing a keg is generally a bad idea.)

Another example of trespass on public property is when you've specifically been banned from the area. This occurs in public housing projects, for example, or in instances where you've caused trouble before. If you're a real troublemaker, you might get slapped with a restraining order. Going against these orders is a fast way to get arrested.

> **YOU'RE NOT WELCOME, BUDDY:** Can the government ban you, personally, from public property? A recent Supreme Court decision upheld the trespass charge against "Gatsby" for trespassing onto Whitcomb Court, a public housing facility in Richmond, Virginia. Because this particular public housing facility was known as a hotbed of drug dealing, the Housing Authority enacted a law stating that nonresidents could

be arrested for entering if they didn't have valid business there. Gatsby, previously arrested for trespassing and damaging the property, argued that the law restricted his First Amendment freedom of association. The Supreme Court disagreed, recognizing that the Housing Authority had a legitimate interest in protecting its residents.

Getting Caught

First of all, most property owners have a "reasonable right" to protect their property and their family if threatened. What this means for you is that if a property owner thinks that you're going to be dangerous, he can take action. And that action depends on you.

Two things are going to make your situation worse: being under the influence and being armed. If you're twitchy and irrational, you're going to scare the shit out of that poor landowner. The only thing worse than that is showing off your hunting knife or your Luger. Landowners have a right to protect their property with force, and if you're armed and dangerous, they have a right to use deadly force to protect themselves and their family.

Street Law Concept #45: Deadly Force

Deadly force is a physical action that is likely to cause death or really bad injuries. A property owner can't use deadly force to protect just his property, but he can use deadly force if he thinks he or his family is in trouble.

In Case You Get Hurt . . .

Ever heard of a case like this? A trespasser steals onto the landowner's property. There's a jagged hole right near the fence. The trespasser falls in, gets hurt, and sues the landowner for causing his injuries. And guess what? He wins. One of the reasons the trespasser can win is because the court found that it was foreseeable that someone might end up on that property—not just trespassers, but neighborhood kids or lost hikers, for example. The landowner has a duty to keep his property safe for guests and reasonably safe even for trespassers. However, (a) it has to be a situation that the landlord at least negligently failed to fix, and (b) it has to be something that could have hurt innocent victims, not just your thieving self. For example, the landlord will be held liable if he sets up a gun to automatically shoot if the back door opens at night. He won't, however, be liable if you're a burglar and you fall through his roof—unless other circumstances are involved.

PROTEST CAN WORK: A centuries-old oak tree (Old Glory) in Santa Clarita, California, was slated for demolition until environmentalist "Tarzan" came to its rescue. Tarzan camped out in the tree's branches for seventy days to prevent the tree from being destroyed. The building company sued him for trespassing and libel, but dropped its suit a year later, stating that it wanted to work to preserve the tree. Now the tree is slated to be replanted in a local park, and everyone is happy.

Roommates

The law doesn't like to interfere between two people living together. This can get tricky if you break up with your live-in boyfriend or are trying to oust an annoying roommate. Landlord-tenant laws vary wildly from jurisdiction to jurisdiction, but in general, there are no hard-and-fast laws dealing with roommates.

The bad news first: if your annoying roommate pays rent, lives in the apartment, or even just significantly contributed to the possessions in the apartment, he's probably going to be able to stay—even if his name is not on the lease. This varies from state to state, but for the most part, the police cannot charge someone for criminal trespass for simply and peaceably refusing to leave the place where he lives. Even a landlord can't get him to do that for you. The roommate does, however, have to have some proof of his involvement in the apartment—rent receipts, for example, or check stubs.

The good news is that virtually every state has civil remedies to help you evict an unwanted roommate. The procedures vary, and the roommate can fight it, but generally there are ways to resolve the dispute without too much bloodshed. Furthermore, if the unwanted roommate starts destroying property or causing a ruckus, you can call the cops for that. If the roommate threatens you, you can even try to get a restraining order.

Once the roommate is gone, don't start a garage sale of his or her possessions. The roommate still has a right to collect her things. If you can't stand the sight of her, don't be home when she comes to pick up her stuff. But don't try refusing her entry to get her stuff—it'll cause more trouble than you want and make you look pretty bad.

Chart 12: Penalties for Breaking and Entering or Trespass

In the following instances, the assumption is that (a) you didn't steal anything or show an intent to steal anything,

(b) you didn't use violence or hurt anyone, and (c) you didn't destroy any valuable property (although the latter will probably just add to your fine).

City	Maximum Fine	Maximum Jail Time
Los Angeles	$1,000	6 months
District of Columbia	$1,000	6 months
Miami	$500	2 months
Chicago (unoccupied building)	$2,500	1 year
Las Vegas	$1,000	6 months
New York	$500	3 months
Dallas	$2,000	6 months

NUISANCE

Nuisance occurs when someone does something that interferes with the use of land or a public place. For example, you might have the greatest garden in the world, but you won't want to go there if your neighbor is burning tires in his backyard. That smell he's creating is a nuisance, and it's illegal. And if your dog barks day and night without stopping, that noise is a nuisance for your neighbor.

There are two kinds of nuisance.

Street Law Concept #46: Public vs. Private Nuisance

All nuisances are judged according to community standards. If you live in a commune of punk rock musicians, then your guitar solos probably won't be considered a nuisance. In any other neighborhood, at midnight, it probably will be.

● A *public* nuisance disturbs the whole community, rather than just one person. An example is dumping sewage into a neighborhood lake.

● A *private* nuisance disturbs only a small number of people. This usually occurs when you're making a racket and keeping your neighbor up at night.

Noise

The most common type of nuisance is noise. Whether it's your dog or your boom box, whether you're at home or on the road, creating unreasonable noise so that people can't enjoy themselves will get you cited for creating a nuisance. Yes, you do have to be trying to make the noise, so the noise from a car accident won't do it. But you don't have to be trying to disturb someone. You just have to be loud.

Most of the time, you have to be making a consistent racket. If you've got to be loud and can't help it, make it quick. That way, when the cops show up, you can look at them blankly and say, "What chain saw, Officer?"

One way to head off a nuisance charge is to let your neighbors know what's going on. If you're going to have a party, warn them. This won't prevent the cops from showing up on your doorstep, but the neighbors might put up with it for a little while longer before making the call. It's almost always more acceptable to make a racket during daylight hours, and the quicker the better.

Other Property Nuisance

How you take care of your property affects others. If you blow your leaves into your neighbor's yard, you're interfering with their property. (The cops might bust you for trespass or nuisance, depending on the laws of the state.) There are a million ways to annoy your neighbor, and just one to keep him off your back: communicate. If he's the ultrasensitive sort who whines about everything, he may not convince the cops that you're creating a real nuisance. If he's normal, you might be able to reach a compromise.

> **NOT EXACTLY NEIGHBORLY:** "Michelangelo" considered himself an artist. The neighborhood considered him a nuisance. Michelangelo covered his yard with junk and refuse, attracting rats and flies. His masterpiece? A life-size replica of his buttocks. Neighbors complained the mess was actually driving property values down. Finally, Michelangelo was convicted of criminal littering—a third-degree felony in Florida— and faces up to five years in prison.

Your pets can be a nuisance, too. Pick up after Fido, and keep him on a leash whenever he's off your property—especially if he's got a temper. If he barks day and night, do something about it: get a trainer or a muzzle or whatever it takes. And don't encourage him to fight with other animals. (Pitting animals against each other is a crime. As it should be.)

HEE-HAW, BROTHER: "Pugsley Addams" lived in a trailer between his dad's property and his uncle's ("Uncle Fester's") property. After Daddy died, a dispute arose regarding the exact boundaries of the properties. Lacking any interest in keeping the peace, Uncle Fester not only built a fence blocking Pugsley's driveway, but decided that he wanted to raise hogs there as well. Pugsley argued that the hogs in front of his trailer (along with empty paint cans and half a toilet) created a nuisance and made it impossible for him to sell his home. Weeding through complicated familial issues, the court found that the hogs did constitute a nuisance, as the odor and flies would bother any normal person. The court also noted evidence that the Uncle Fester clan had acted maliciously, as they could have put the hogs elsewhere.

PROPERTY LAWS

The number one type of arrest for first timers (and juveniles) is a property offense: theft, burglary, vandalism, etc. Here's a rundown of property offenses, including personal property (theft and burglary, damaging personal goods, etc.) and public property (graffiti, vandalism, property damage). Our one caveat is this: if you use violence or intimidation of any kind, you're on your own. A small scuffle in a bar is far different from bullying someone to hand over his wallet.

Theft

In the world of law, theft falls into one of two categories: grand or petit (also known as petty theft by those who think the French term is too sissy).

> **Street Law Concept #47: Grand Theft vs. Petit Theft**
> The difference between grand and petit theft depends on the value of what has been stolen. Many states draw the line at $400. Grand theft is usually a felony, while petit theft is generally a misdemeanor.

Note that law is notoriously unsentimental; even if someone steals your grandmother's precious family photographs, collected over a century, it's petit theft unless you can prove they were worth over $400. It's also no good if the stolen stuff will be worth more in the future—a rare painting, for example. Generally, the measure of theft occurs when the property is stolen. So even if the artist who painted your stolen portrait dies in two months, tripling the value of the painting, it's still a petit theft if the portrait was worth $399.99 at the time of the robbery. (Note: there is some room for argument here, but not much.) And finally, it doesn't matter that you intended to steal something worth less than $400. If you grab someone's money clip and it has $401, then welcome to the world of grand theft.

This distinction is important because grand theft is a serious business and can lead to felony time. Petty theft is usually a misdemeanor. Either way, you'll probably be required to make some kind of restitution.

CLEVER, BUT NOT CLEVER ENOUGH: Students at Massachusetts's Newton South High School knew their annual scavenger hunt might get them into trouble. After all, some of the ways you could score points included vandalism, theft, and possession of weed. However, to fool the authorities, the class of 2003 created two lists of items for the hunt—the real one, and a PG-rated version in case the cops gave them trouble. Sadly, enterprising cops got ahold of both lists and are preparing to charge dozens of students with multiple misdemeanors.

Shoplifting

The most common type of theft (far more common than pickpocketing or purse-snatching) is shoplifting, which has gotten a lot harder in the technological age. To deter those interested in the five-fingered discount, shopkeepers have a few tricks up their sleeve:

- *The security clamp:* that big clunky plastic thing that they need a special gadget to remove. It will tear a hole in your clothes unless you know how to get it off, and that usually requires a special tool.
- *The price tag:* the bigger the price tag—not just in price, but in size—the more trouble you can get into. Many price tags have a little electronic sticker inside that works on a magnetic or radio frequency. Even price stickers can have this. There's virtually no way to be sure.
- *Security cameras:* don't assume they're not there because you can't spot them. There's nothing more embarrassing than vehemently denying you did the deed, only to be faced with a video of yourself—well, doing the deed.
- *Mirrors:* those curved mirrors enable cashiers to see down different aisles. Sometimes they have cameras behind them as well.

All in all, shoplifting isn't as easy as it used to be, and you should be really careful if you're planning a heist. Who knows what you might be charged with?

MAYOR MAYBE: "Grandma Moses" was caught shoplifting at Wal-Mart in Granger, Iowa. Her haul? Four lithium batteries, cigarettes, and a wristwatch. Big deal, right? Well, a search of her person revealed ephedrine, a pipe, a vial and a bag with residue, and a glass lighter. And, oh, yeah, ephedrine and lithium batteries contain ingredients for making methamphetamine . . . which Grandma had been charged with three years earlier. Cops charged Grandma with a variety of "possession with intent" charges, as well as violating her probation from the previous meth charge. Should they have gone easy on her? Well, Grandma has quite a history to work with: she's also suspected of embezzling city funds when she was *mayor* of Granger in 2001.

However, stores have to follow a certain procedure when dealing with shoplifters. The security guard cannot usually search your bags unless he has your permission, or unless he actually saw you take the item in plain view and can identify it. You can, however, be detained for a reasonable time. (Where does he get that right? Many states have "merchant's statutes," which remove liability from store owners who suspect someone of shoplifting. Or it can be a "citizen's arrest." However, he should not use abusive language or humiliate you in front of other customers.

Street Law Concept #48: Citizen's Arrest

A citizen's arrest is an arrest by a private individual who isn't affiliated with law enforcement. It can be anybody, but is usually only valid for certain people (such as security guards in stores) or in special circumstances (when you're trying to stop a felony from happening, or the criminal is getting away).

Stealing as a Prank

Kids these days! They go from stealing gum balls to stealing the goat from the 4-H Club. Who can guess this week's trendy frat-boy prank? But one seems never to die in popularity: sign stealing. The sign outside the kosher deli, the Deer Crossing sign, the advertisement for teeth whitening. Somehow, a startling number of these signs end up in dorm rooms, and damned if anyone knows why.

Sign stealing can lead to serious trouble. After all, those signs are there for a reason. Generally the theft of a public sign is a much greater crime than stealing a private sign, since a missing public sign can affect public safety. Under no circumstances should you steal stop signs, road signs, signs signaling hazards or dangers, or any type of railroad sign.

A NOT-SO-PETTY THEFT: In 1996, "Hamlet" was driving his car down a street in Tampa, Florida, when a tractor trailer slammed into the car, killing Hamlet and his two passengers immediately. The police found a stop sign on the ground, which should have prevented the accident if it hadn't been removed. A little investigation revealed that "Claudius," "Polonius," and "Gertrude" had spent the night before drinking, carousing around town, and stealing traffic signs. Though they denied stealing—or uprooting—this particular stop sign, the court found the three guilty of manslaughter and sentenced them each to fifteen years in prison. The defendants appealed and, in 2001, got the sentence overturned because of prosecutorial error. Then they got really lucky—the DA decided that he wasn't going to retry them, and the three narrowly missed doing felony time. They were, however, sentenced to five years of probation and 250 hours of community service to talk to teenagers about their experiences.

Chart 13: Penalties for Petty Theft

The following penalties are for the lowest level of petit theft. Anything more than the dollar amount will get you harsher penalties. And anything involving force, breaking and entering, intimidation, or any other crime—along with your theft—will get you harsher penalties. Also, the fines listed are usually in addition to paying restitution for the property you nabbed.

City	Maximum Fine	Maximum Jail Time
Los Angeles (under $400)	$1,000	6 months
District of Columbia (under $250)	$1,000	6 months
Miami (under $100)	$500	2 months
Chicago (under $300)	$2,500	1 year
Las Vegas (under $250)	$1,000	6 months
New York (under $1,000)	$1,000	1 year
Dallas ($50–$500)	$2,000	6 months

Burglary

If you have dreams of being one of those David Niven/Cary Grant–type cat burglars, just remember this—most burglary raps include felony time. Cops take burglars seriously, since people need to feel safe in their homes.

Street Law Concept #49: Burglary

Burglary is the crime of breaking into a building (or "dwelling") with the intent to commit a felony. The felony can be anything, not just stealing stuff. You've got to do both for a burglary charge: it isn't enough just to break in (which is a different charge, already covered).

HOLY PANTY RAID, BATMAN!: Some people collect stamps. Others collect coins. "Uriah Heep" of Menomonie, Wisconsin, collected thong underwear. Only one problem—he liked to steal them from women's bedrooms. Cops arrested the budding collector in April 2003 for breaking and entering into a house and, when they searched the suspect's house, found 850 pairs of ladies' thong underwear, stuffed into shoe boxes, dressers, briefcases, you name it. The underwear enthusiast claimed that he'd gotten the panties from various panty raids, but the cops booked him for burglary and criminal damage anyway.

Chart 14: Penalties for Burglary

Burglary is almost always a felony offense. The law also accounts for differences between breaking into an *inhabited* dwelling and one that isn't. This doesn't mean that there has to be someone sleeping upstairs—just that someone has to be living/working there, as opposed to the building's being abandoned or not in use. *Occupied* means someone was actually in the building at the time you were breaking in. *Dwelling* means a house or home, as opposed to an office building.

CITY	MAXIMUM FINE	MAXIMUM JAIL TIME
Los Angeles (inhabited building)	Not listed	2–6 years
District of Columbia (occupied)	Not listed	5–30 years
Miami (all dwellings)	$10,000	15 years
Chicago (nonresidential)	$25,000	3–7 years
Las Vegas	$10,000	1–10 years
New York (not a dwelling)	$5,000	3–7 years
Dallas (not inhabited)	$10,000	6 months to 2 years

Vandalism

The official term for vandalism is *criminal mischief*.

Street Law Concept #50: Criminal Mischief/Vandalism
Criminal mischief is when you damage property that you don't own. The amount of damage usually determines your punishment. If the damage includes racial/gender/ethnic slurs, then the criminal mischief turns into a bias crime. Many states have special hate-crime or bias-crime statutes.

Therefore, feel free to beat the crap out of your own possessions, but once you move into damaging other people's property (or public property), the law will be unhappy. Here are some common types of criminal mischief:

- Toilet-papering your neighbor's house
- Egging, soaping, or smashing windows
- Letting air out of car tires
- Destroying graveyard property (if unhappy ghosts don't get you first, that is)
- Carving your name into doors or on the sides of cars
- Covering school hallways with shaving cream
- Most graffiti (but see below)

Basically, any prank that you can think of is covered under criminal mischief. What you get depends on the amount of dollar damage you caused. Toilet papering someone's house is minor league compared to scratching up someone's Mercedes with your keys. Not only will you probably have to pay for the damage to the car, but you'll probably get a pretty stiff punishment—maybe even a felony charge, depending on the amount of damage.

Graffiti
Don't get us wrong—graffiti is criminal mischief, whether you use a can of spray paint, conventional paint, or a Magic Marker. But for many people, graffiti is a combination of free speech and artistic invention. Many writers (as graffiti artists are known) risk jail and prison fines to "write" their vision onto blank city walls, hoping that their words and their pictures will be seen as art.

Street Law Concept #51: Graffiti

Graffiti is the painting or marking of large flat surfaces, most commonly walls of buildings. The difference between graffiti and art is that graffiti is almost always done without permission from the building's owner. The essential purpose of graffiti is to make a statement or create an artwork that is visible to (though not always understood by) the general public.

Unfortunately, it probably won't. It doesn't matter what you're writing up there—gang signs, a poem by Byron, an ode to the mayor—if you don't have permission from the wall's owner, it's illegal. For some, the very illegality of graffiti is the point—who wants to play around with conventional art? If this is your view, then remember—cops have a right to arrest you, no matter how good your artwork is. Professional writers take many precautions regarding safety (using masks to prevent fume inhalation), laws (working at night and never using their real names), and artistic integrity (having the design planned in advance).

Whatever you decide, remember this: obscenity or profanity will cause more trouble and encourage the cops to work extrahard to hunt you down. Some cities have "graffiti walls" that are intended specifically for graffiti writers.

NOW ALL I NEED IS AN AGENT: Muralists shouldn't lose all hope. In 1980, Shell Oil commissioned a twelve-hundred-foot mural for one of its California stations. In 1988, the gas station tore the mural down to make way for a parking lot. The irate artists sued, claiming that their work was protected by the Art Preservation

Act. The act states that a "work of art" cannot arbitrarily be destroyed because there is a public interest in preserving the integrity of fine artwork. Shell claimed that murals were not considered fine art, but the appellate court disagreed. They pointed out the act should be broadly interpreted to include murals, and Shell had an obligation to the artists. Don't get too hopeful—these artists were legally commissioned, and the court specifically noted that graffiti was *not* included in the act.

Chart 15: Penalties for Criminal Mischief

Criminal mischief includes, but is not limited to, any of the above misbehaviors. Just because it isn't listed doesn't mean it won't get you arrested. The dollar values listed are the maximum amount of property damage for the listed sentence.

City	Maximum Fine	Maximum Jail Time
Los Angeles (under $400)	$1,000	1 year
District of Columbia (any amount)	$250–1,000	6 months
Miami (under $200)	$500	2 months
Chicago (under $300)	$2,500	1 year
Las Vegas (amount not listed; maybe under $250)	$1,000	6 months

CITY	MAXIMUM FINE	MAXIMUM JAIL TIME
New York (under $250)	$1,000	1 year
Dallas ($50–500)	$2,000	6 months

ALCOHOL

Your twelve-year-old niece steals some. Your eighty-year-old grandfather guzzles it. It gives you a buzz and it's legal—what's not to like about alcohol? Many folks who would never ever smoke a joint or even a cigarette drink themselves into a coma every Saturday night. Sure, you can get away with a lot more with alcohol possession than with illegal narcotics, but don't go crazy yet—you still have some laws to follow.

Underage Drinking

Whatever the government says, most people consider the age of twenty-one a general "guideline" for drinking, rather than a hard-and-fast rule. Few young adults wait until then to have their first drink, and many have already gotten their hardest drinking out of the way by the time twenty-one rolls around. And as much as some people like to tell you it starts in college, research by those big important-scientist types indicates that drinking usually starts in high school—if not junior high.

Whatever the norm is, however, the law likes to stick to the old "twenty-one and over" routine. Underage drinking is usually a violation or a misdemeanor and can come along with a variety of punishments. There's usually a fine. There can also be community service, required educational seminars on the dangers of underage drinking, and in most cases, you will have your driver's license suspended. You will be liable for any and all damages you did while you were drunk. Selling alcohol or being drunk at school can get you expelled. (And you're in more trouble if you aren't actually attending the school or you're an adult.)

DOUBLE YOUR PLEASURE: Jenna and Barbara Bush clearly know how to party. Two weeks after being busted for underage drinking, Jenna Bush was busted for using someone else's driver's license in an attempt to get more booze. Her sister, Barbara, was better at the fake ID thing than Jenna—she'd gotten the booze, but cops busted her for possession of alcohol by a minor. A little over a year earlier, cops had questioned Barbara for her involvement in a raucous party at Harvard Square (with lots of underage drinking).

Drunk Driving

Drunk driving looks really really bad on your record, can result in heavy punishment, and, oh, yeah, it kills. Nothing destroys a good buzz like, well, death.

Street Law Concept #52: Blood Alcohol Concentration
Also known as BAC. This is a measure of ethanol (the stuff in alcohol that gets you drunk) in the blood. It's usually measured in terms of grams per hundred milliliters.

In general, traffic cops are trained to look for certain indicators that a driver might be under the influence. Here are a few: following a car too closely, making really wide turns, weaving or swerving, sudden stops or abrupt turns, really slow driving, jerking on your brakes, or almost hitting an object. If you're in a car and your driver is doing this, just say no and make him pull over. If you don't do it, a cop probably will anyway.

Alcohol Impairment Chart

Men

Approximate Blood Alcohol Percentage

Drinks	|←			Body Weight in Pounds				→|	
	100	120	140	160	180	200	220	240	
0	.00	.00	.00	.00	.00	.00	.00	.00	Only Safe Driving Limit
1	.04	.03	.03	.02	.02	.02	.02	.02	Impairment Begins
2	.08	.06	.05	.05	.04	.04	.03	.03	
3	.11	.09	.08	.07	.06	.06	.05	.05	Driving Skills Significantly Affected
4	.15	.12	.11	.09	.08	.08	.07	.06	
5	.19	.16	.13	.12	.11	.09	.09	.08	
6	.23	.19	.16	.14	.13	.11	.10	.09	Possible Criminal Penalties
7	.26	.22	.19	.16	.15	.13	.12	.11	Legally Intoxicated
8	.30	.25	.21	.19	.17	.15	.14	.13	
9	.34	.28	.24	.21	.19	.17	.15	.14	Criminal Penalties
10	.38	.31	.27	.23	.21	.19	.17	.16	

Substract .01 for each 40 minutes of drinking.

One drink is 1.25 oz. of 80 proof liquor, 12 oz. of beer, or 5 oz. of table wine.

Women

Approximate Blood Alcohol Percentage

Drinks   Body Weight in Pounds

Drinks	90	100	120	140	160	180	200	220	240	
0	0.00	.00	.00	.00	.00	.00	.00	.00	.00	Only Safe Driving Limit
1	.05	.05	.04	.03	.03	.03	.02	.02	.02	Impairment Begins
2	.10	.09	.08	.07	.06	.05	.05	.04	.04	
3	.15	.14	.11	.10	.09	.08	.07	.06	.06	Driving Skills Significantly Affected
4	.20	.18	.15	.13	.11	.10	.09	.08	.08	
5	.25	.23	.19	.16	.14	.13	.11	.10	.09	Possible Criminal Penalties
6	.30	.27	.23	.19	.17	.15	.14	.12	.11	Legally Intoxicated
7	.35	.32	.27	.23	.20	.18	.16	.14	.13	
8	.40	.36	.30	.26	.23	.20	.18	.17	.15	————
9	.45	.41	.34	.29	.26	.23	.20	.19	.17	Criminal Penalties
10	.51	.45	.38	.32	.28	.25	.23	.21	.19	

Subtract .01 for each 40 minutes of drinking.

One drink is 1.25 oz. of 80 proof liquor, 12 oz. of beer, or 5 oz. of table wine.

Source: National Commission Against Drunk Driving, 2003

Rights of the Drunk Driver
If you are pulled over for drunk driving, you have a couple

of options. In many states, you don't have to answer any questions about what you've had to drink, and you're not required to take any type of sobriety tests. Yes, you heard that right. However, it's not that simple. If a cop is asking you to take a sobriety test, he might've already made up his mind about whether you're drunk. Cops are trained to look for certain things when they suspect someone of being drunk: flushed or sweaty face, unsteadiness, inappropriate laughter or anger, etc. You can refuse the sobriety test or a Breathalyzer, but the cops can still haul you in—they don't need a test to arrest you. In some cases, when you refuse a test and it's later proven that you were drunk, you could be facing harsher penalties than if you'd taken it when asked.

Then there's the "rising blood alcohol concentration" issue. Remember, it's illegal to be caught driving with a blood alcohol level over some limit. However, it can take anywhere from forty-five minutes to two hours for alcohol to get absorbed into your blood.

Street Law Concept #53: Rising BAC (Blood Alcohol Content)
A legal defense to drunk driving. The more time elapsed between being pulled over and being tested, the more problems the police will have in determining exactly how drunk you were at the time of the driving.

For example, if you get tested four hours after being pulled over, and your blood alcohol level is at the exact legal limit (let's say 0.10), then you can argue that at the time of being pulled over, you must, logically, have been under that limit—say, only 0.07. For this reason, cops want to do tests as soon as possible.

Getting It

Believe it or not, it's legal to make your own wine or beer—but only if it's for personal consumption. If you think of it as a get-rich-quick scheme, forget about it. The authorities will come down on you hard if you don't have a license.

It is not legal to make any type of spirit—vodka, Everclear, whatever—for either personal use or sale. You need a license and have to go through a lengthy application process.

As for buying it, a bartender can refuse to serve you when he thinks you've had too much. This is because the bar can be liable for the damage you cause if they continued to serve you even after you were clearly intoxicated. In real life, it's rare for a bartender or waiter to stop serving someone, but she can still make the call. If you argue, you can be thrown out.

JEEZ, MY MOM JUST BAKED ME A CAKE: For her son's sweet sixteen birthday party in 2002, "Ma Barker" of Olympia, Washington, went all out. Not only did she provide paintball guns and a ride on a "gyroscope," but she also welcomed her son's friends with booze, weed, and a friendly stripper (who may or may not have given the birthday boy a blow job). Some of the lucky underage party guests threw up from too much booze, but a good time was had by all . . . until some of the neighborhood parents found out. Ma Barker and her husband were charged with a felony and a variety of misdemeanors (including providing alcohol to minors) and paid a hefty $15,000 fine.

Open Container Laws

Thirty-six states have open container laws.

Street Law Concept #54: Open Container Laws

These laws regulate when and where you can be with an open container of alcohol (including beer and wine). Most of these laws do not allow alcohol on public streets or in a moving car (even if the driver is not drinking).

Various states make different distinctions—some say no open containers only in the front car seat, while others don't really care where it's found. It doesn't matter if the driver is sober or not. It's a tough law. You can try transferring your alcohol into soda cans, or something like that, but the cop will probably smell the alcohol if you've been drinking a lot.

In many states, you are not allowed to drink in public. That means no crossing the street with a beer in your hand. This is the primary reason that those nice homeless drunks drink out of brown paper bags.

ASSAULT

In some situations, a calm conversation and pacifist intervention may just not do it. Particularly if you've been drinking or are generally just out of it and some guy picks a fight. Then, you may want to raise your fists—or maybe just one—to show the lout whom he's dealing with.

> **Street Law Concept #55: Assault vs. Battery**
>
> Contrary to popular belief, assault isn't when you beat some-
> one up. Simple assault occurs even when you threaten some-
> one enough to make him believe that you're going to harm him.
> If there is an injury, then it's minor. Battery is "offensive touch-
> ing," which can be as small as that of a hangnail. Usually you'll
> be charged with assault and battery if you're in a fight.

The golden rule of any altercation, if you end up in one, is this: don't pick anything up. This includes wineglasses, ketchup bottles, chair legs, napkin dispensers, etc. Do not pick anything up. Resist the urge to arm yourself. Scream like a little girl and run away, but do not use a weapon. Without a weapon, you will probably be charged with simple assault and/or battery.

Injuries

Though regulations vary from state to state, it's usually pretty hard to get an assault and battery charge to hold up in court when your victim doesn't show an injury. Again, this isn't a guarantee; it's just the way that the sometimes overcrowded court system looks at these issues. A vengeful victim can go all the way and try to press criminal charges and start a civil lawsuit against you. He's going to have a hard time with the criminal case if he can't point to a real, physical injury. (Note: hurt feelings and wounded reputation do not count.)

In short, it's easy to get charged with assault, but whether you're actually convicted often depends on the amount of damage you do. Which is a good thing, since it seems that practically everyone gets into a brawl now and then. Even famous people.

REALITY TELEVISION IS BAD FOR YOU: A surprising number of reality television contestants seem to have a flair for trouble. "Beowulf," one of MTV *Real World*'s innumerable participants, got a little too wild at a charity event in Charlotte, North Carolina. After complaining about being paraded like a "sideshow freak," the "star" started biting, scratching, and cursing. Beowulf also threw a punch, which didn't connect, and got hauled off by the cops.

MORE PROOF THAT REALITY TELEVISION IS BAD FOR YOU: "Elizabeth" can be proud—it's not every girl who can appear on MTV's *Real World* and beat up a marine. Yep, you heard us. The petite female bartender jumped marine "Darcy" at Coyote Ugly, a bar in Tampa, Florida, in 2003. Darcy suffered from six long scratches, and Elizabeth was charged with misdemeanor battery.

Assault is not a fun-and-games charge. You don't know how your actions will affect people.

PROOF THAT REALITY TELEVISION IS REALLY BAD FOR YOU: "Tom," a finalist in last year's *American Idol* contest, got disorderly in a public place and punched "Huck" out. Unfortunately, Huck fell backward and hit his head on the pavement. One of Tom's buddies attacked the prone Huck on the ground, and Huck died as a result of his injuries. Tom is only being charged with misdemeanor assault (his buddy is being charged with aggravated assault), but *American Idol* bumped him off the finals list.

The best defense for an assault charge is self-defense.

Street Law Concept #56: Self-Defense

You are allowed to use reasonable force to defend yourself when you legitimately believe that you're physically in danger. It's very, very important that you didn't do anything to create this dangerous situation or make it worse once it started.

You can't use excessive force—that is, you can't use a knife when someone has just shoved you around a little. And you can't throw a punch if all the other guy has done is tell you what a loser you are. And saying "I was too drunk to know any better" is not going to help you with an assault/battery charge. (In life, it rarely helps you with anything.)

Aggravated Assault and Battery

This charge requires that you get a lawyer—fast. Aggravated assault and battery is a serious problem, and you might be charged with a felony.

Street Law Concept #57: Aggravated Assault

Aggravated assault is assault with extra circumstances. These circumstances depend on what state you're in, but they usually include things like waving or using a weapon, assaulting someone while you're trying to commit another crime (like robbery), threatening someone with rape, murder, or really severe injuries, or actually causing serious injury. Generally, if you assault a child or a cop, you'll be charged with aggravated assault.

Note that the meaning of *deadly weapon* can change. A car can be a deadly weapon in the right hands. So can a nice friendly pet. Yes, you are responsible for Fido's actions, so be careful if you're training him to attack on command.

SICKENING: In September 2003, "Macbeth" was released from prison after serving two years of a manslaughter charge. His wife, "Lady Macbeth," will be released in March 2004 for the same charge. Their weapon of choice? Two 120-pound dogs named Hera and Bane. These little puppies tore apart their neighbor "Snow White" in January 2001, right in front of her apartment. In the aftermath of the killing, the Macbeths expressed no remorse, accused Snow of not defending herself, dared the DA to arrest them, refused to answer bestiality allegations, adopted a forty-year-old Aryan Brotherhood convict as their son (or lover, no one knows), and claimed the dogs were harmless. Snow, who was a lesbian, is survived by "Rose Red," her partner of seven years. Rose is suing the Gruesome Twosome in a wrongful death suit, usually reserved for traditional spouses.

The above example can go either way. Mess with your neighbor's dog, and you'll be facing serious criminal charges of animal cruelty—not to mention a definite civil lawsuit from Fido's owner. And since torturing animals is one of the signs of a budding serial killer, you'll probably start receiving extra-close attention from police officers everywhere. If you feel the urge, close this book and call a shrink.

Additionally, if you assault certain types of people, the penalty goes through the roof. Everyone knows that assaulting a police officer is a serious offense. But many states increase penalties for assaults against cabdrivers, emergency technicians, doctors, and other government workers.

Defensive Weapons

Some people like to be extra-careful. That's where defensive weapons—pepper spray, Mace, Tasers, stun guns, etc.—come in. While you might feel safer walking down dangerous streets, you should remember this: any weapon you carry on you can be taken away and used against you.

Pepper spray is legal in all fifty states, but some states have guidelines regarding the size and age of canisters (yes, pepper spray can expire), as well as ingredient regulations. Stun guns are illegal in some states, and even in some cities. Furthermore, certain people aren't allowed to possess these types of weapons. A minor cannot possess Mace, for example. Neither can some felons. Our advice is to check the laws of your state and city before you purchase any defensive weapons.

States Where Stun Guns Are Illegal

Hawaii
Massachusetts
Michigan
New Jersey
New York
Rhode Island
Wisconsin

Though they're rarely considered deadly weapons (as knives and guns are), defensive weapons are still weapons. Use one as a prank, and you'll be punished—from fines (usually in the thousands of dollars) to jail time (occasionally felony time). Maliciously attack someone with your stun gun and it's aggravated assault. And if you spray some guy chasing after you in the parking garage—only to find out he's the valet trying to return your keys—you might face criminal charges and/or a civil lawsuit if you can't prove you were legitimately frightened of an attack.

Given heightened national security, you won't be able to take your stun gun or pepper spray everywhere. You probably won't be able to take it with you into government buildings, for example. The best guideline is to look out for those security checkpoints where your bags may be searched, since officials might confiscate your weapon if you try to get through. When flying, you should always check your defensive weapons in with your baggage.

Chart 16: Penalties for Simple Assault/Battery

The following punishments are for the lowest level of simple assault and battery. If you use a weapon, cause a serious injury, or have any of the above aggravating circumstances, the penalty will be much higher.

City	Maximum Fine	Maximum Jail Time
Los Angeles	$1,000	6 months
District of Columbia	$1,000	6 months
Miami	$500	2 months
Chicago	$1,500	1 month
Las Vegas	$1,000	6 months
New York	$1,000	1 year
Dallas	$4,000	1 year

CONCLUSION

This chapter is a grab bag of violations and misdemeanors, with the occasional felony thrown in. Many, many other offenses are covered by local, city, or municipal codes, which are peculiar in their own ways. It's a little hard to give you the inside scoop when there are, well, thousands of them.

Still, everyone likes to engage in mischief now and then. If no one gets hurt and everyone has fun, then what's the problem? Just be sure that your idea of fun isn't the law's idea of a crime—or if it is, at least try to keep it off the police radar. If that doesn't work, you'll need to know about dealing with the cops—because they're probably heading toward your door.

CHAPTER 4

They're On to Me: Dealing with the Cops

INTRODUCTION

This chapter should not be interpreted as an attack on decent law enforcement officials. But, just as there are three kinds of people, there are three kinds of cops: the good, the bad, and the ugly.

Good cops are heroes. They're the reason everyone can walk the streets at night. They're whom people turn to when things go bad. The good cops are doing their job in an honest, ethical, and dedicated manner. It's a hard job and everyone relies on them, even when they're on the wrong side of the law.

Bad cops either don't know the law or they don't care. They'll give you grief because they don't know any better, and then they'll complain when their behavior is questioned. Bad cops are the bane of the justice system; they run around like Keystone Kops to hide that they don't know what they're doing.

Ugly cops are downright dangerous. These cops know what they're doing is wrong. They plant evidence, make up stories, take bribes. Ugly cops arrest people because of the color of their skin and are not above manhandling a suspect. They play by their own rules and don't really care about the law they're supposed to be upholding. These cops shouldn't be cops; most of them should be behind bars.

The trouble, however, lies in figuring out what kind of cop you're dealing with. And that isn't always easy. You might get one of the good guys, who's going to do his job fairly and firmly. You might get an uneducated bully who gets off on the power of the badge. Or you might get someone who needs you to be guilty even if you haven't done anything and isn't above using violence to make his point. In the first five minutes of being questioned, you just won't know. It's important to be calm and courteous to all police.

That said, there are a lot of techniques to handling the cops. None of these are guaranteed to prevent an arrest, but they will give you a fighting chance to stay out of real trouble.

LEVELS OF QUESTIONING

When is a question an interrogation? When do you have to answer it? What happens if you don't? Can you just walk away? There are a million questions about questioning, but to make sense of the process, you have to start by identifying the various levels of questioning that the police engage in. The "official" terms vary from state to state, so this is just a rundown of the more general categories. And remember, even before your arrest, you always have *the right to remain silent*.

The Right to Inquire

> **Street Law Concept #58: The Common Law Right to Inquire**
> Also known as casual encounter or a friendly conversation. This is the least intrusive level of police questioning. It can cover any topic, and you are generally not obliged to answer if you don't want to.

You're walking down the street, and a cop stops you and asks a question. It might be about the time, it might be about your jacket, it might be about what you're doing standing outside the bank. Cops don't need much by way of suspicion to stop and ask you what you're doing. This will not be a formal question—it might be casual, offhand, as if he's asking you whether the Yankees won today.

This is almost always in public, and the cop should not move you to another location (unless you're in the middle of the street or something like that). At a slightly more intense level of inquiry, a cop can pat you down. A pat-down occurs when a cop pats your outer clothing to search for suspicious bulges—guns, drugs, etc. You shouldn't have to take off any clothing for this. Generally, at this stage, a pat-down should only occur if the cop is worried that you might have a weapon on you. However, they're not going to tell you what they're looking for. An example of a pat-down on the federal level is airport screening, when they run that wand thing over you.

A cop may also ask you general questions about your behavior. You are not required to answer these questions— with one caveat. If a cop feels you are loitering, she might ask you questions about what business you have in the area. If you decide not to answer these questions, you could get a loitering citation.

The right to inquire is the right of the cop to detain you momentarily if he thinks some unusual activity is afoot. He doesn't have to suspect a crime. So remember, even though you have *the right to remain silent,* you don't necessarily have the right to walk away. In fact, even if you're totally innocent, this is a bad idea—it'll just make him more suspicious. (There's nothing wrong with asking if you can go, however.)

Reasonable Suspicion

> **Street Law Concept #59: Reasonable Suspicion**
> With reasonable suspicion, the officer suspects that criminal activity is afoot nearby and you have information. He doesn't necessarily suspect that you're involved or guilty, but he is detaining you to get some answers. Something about you makes them suspicious that a crime has been or will be committed.

If the right to inquire seems fluid, you'll love the concept of reasonable suspicion. With reasonable suspicion, the spotlight is on you, not on some "general criminal activity in the area." At the reasonable suspicion level, you are being detained. Not just for a few seconds, as in the inquiry level. You're not sure you're allowed to walk away. Some people state that they're in a hurry and ask if they can leave. If the answer is no, then the cop has a reasonable suspicion that you know something about some criminal activity.

Whether a cop has reasonable suspicion is not dependent on just one fact. Courts have ruled that cops have to look at the whole picture. Therefore, many factors contribute to reasonable suspicion, including the neighborhood you're in and your behavior. This includes anonymous tips.

REASON TO BE NICE TO YOUR NEIGHBORS: Undercover officer "Mina" received an anonymous tip about a local dealer named "Vlad." Pretending to be a "friend,"

Mina called Vlad and told him the cops were onto his drug-dealing ways. Vlad was just rushing out of the house when a waiting Mina stopped him and asked him to consent to a search. Not having read this book, he did and was promptly arrested for cocaine found on his back porch. At court, Vlad argued that the anonymous tip was insufficient for Officer Mina's investigative stop. The court agreed . . . but found that in the "totality of the circumstances," Mina had enough for reasonable suspicion. Their deciding factor? Vlad's suspicious reaction to the phone call.

At this level, a cop has a right to conduct a general stop-and-frisk of your clothing. He may pat you down. His purpose is still to search for weapons—to protect himself—but if he finds any suspicious bulges, the search can get more intense.

Probable Cause

> **Street Law Concept #60: Probable Cause**
> With probable cause, the police officer believes that a crime has been or will be committed, and that you are responsible in some way.

A cop needs probable cause for an arrest. He usually needs probable cause for a thorough search of your person. (More details on searches later.) Like reasonable suspicion, probable cause is a slippery concept, and the cop has to look at the whole picture, including his own information. Needless to say, police hunches are not enough.

So, what is? The smell of marijuana emanating from

your clothes. A tip from an informant naming you as a suspect. Being caught in the act, or soon after the act, with incriminating evidence in your hands. Generally, probable cause means that the cop knows a crime has been committed and reasonably suspects you had something to do with it. With probable cause, a cop can and probably will arrest you.

> **TO THE MOON, ALICE!**: When "Scarlett O'Hara" decided she was leaving boyfriend "Rhett Butler," she got as far as the car. And then he picked up the car and dumped it on a truck. Then, to really make his point, he dangled another car on top of hers. Is he Superman? Not exactly. The loving couple lived in a Kansas auto-wrecking yard, and Rhett used a front-loader to do his heavy lifting. Problem was, after the charges for aggravated assault were filed, the couple got back together and claimed that the DA didn't have probable cause for Rhett's initial arrest. The higher court disagreed, stating that, despite Scarlett's change of testimony, evidence from other witnesses was sufficient to bring the case to trial.

Okay . . . So What?

So you know the various levels of suspicion. But what does this do for you? It can mean plenty—including dismissal of the charges, even if you're guilty.

If a cop doesn't have reasonable suspicion to detain or search you, your lawyer can argue that the detention or search wasn't legal. An illegal search can be enough to dismiss all charges against you. This goes even if they found a vial of crack and a gun in your pocket. Ditto for probable cause. If a cop arrests you without probable cause, the arrest isn't legal, and you can get off scot-free.

It sounds ridiculous. If the illegal search turned up a real criminal, then who cares, right? Well, those pesky founding fathers did. According to the Constitution, a cop has to follow correct procedures without violating people's basic rights. If he doesn't, then cops everywhere could railroad innocent people into jail through racial profiling, threats, intimidation, and other unfair practices. In other words, Dirty Harry would never get away with it in real life.

However, there's just one glitch: you won't know until after your detention/arrest/search whether the detention/arrest/search was legal. The court and a judge will decide that. Arguing with the cop that he doesn't have the right to stop you is going to accomplish just one thing: piss him off. He's gonna start looking for a reason to suspect you or bust you or *something*. He might just take your attitude as a sign that you want trouble.

THIS AIN'T NO FREE COUNTRY: When his mom's car was stolen, "White Rabbit" of Davenport, Iowa, showed up at the station to inquire about it. The desk sergeant, "Mad Hatter," asked him to leave. Why? Because Rabbit was wearing a black T-shirt with about thirty drawings of marijuana leaves on it. Rabbit, not able to believe his ears, insisted on inquiring about the car—only to be arrested and charged with trespassing. Though the charge was dismissed, Rabbit filed a lawsuit against the police department.

DEALING WITH THE POLICE

This might sound surprising, but many cops—especially in cities—aren't so eager to hassle you. Why? you ask. Mainly because they're going to have to stand by that bust in the station, and possibly in court. It's a lot of paperwork and a lot of time, all of which is wasted if you're not guilty of anything. Moreover, a cop who wastes time hassling you isn't out there catching the real bad guys.

Most cops—good or bad—are savvy enough to know that they're being watched. Newspapers and civil rights groups regularly report on police brutality. A busted cop can lose everything. This doesn't stop misconduct from happening, but it does make many cops think twice.

Of course, this doesn't mean you won't get hassled. The best thing to do is to try to be as inconspicuous as possible and avoid looking suspicious.

Factors and Behaviors That Make a Cop Suspicious

- The neighborhood you're in. No, just walking in a high-crime neighborhood isn't enough for reasonable suspicion. But it's a contributing factor, and it makes it more likely that you'll get stopped
- Nervous or evasive behavior—especially when you see a cop. This includes ignoring an officer's request that you stop, ducking into a building, or especially, trying to run away
- Suspicious bulges in your clothing
- Inconsistent answers to questions
- Physically odd or unruly behavior—stumbling, slurring, shouting, etc.
- Looking into car windows or too closely into shop windows for too long

- Loitering without any apparent purpose—especially if you're sitting or standing on a street corner for a long time
- Wearing a mask or covering your face (note: a scarf in cold weather doesn't count. A ski mask, on the other hand, will get their attention)
- Being in a park after hours—even if it's only to walk your dog
- Huddles of people in shadowy corners
- Tips from informants, and descriptions of recent criminal suspects in the area

THAT'S WHAT FRIENDS ARE FOR?

Can you get in trouble for the friends you keep? Absolutely. Being in the wrong place at the wrong time is unfortunate, but get the law involved and it can be downright scary. Even a good cop has to make judgments about who's breaking the law and who's helping him. The question is—am I responsible for what my friends are doing?

To answer that, here's a basic lesson on accomplices, aiders, and co-conspirators. To simplify things, let's say that your friend Roger is planning to rob a bank. Roger is considered the "principal" of the crime, or the primary criminal.

Street Law Concept #61: Accomplice

An accomplice is someone who helps with the crime. In fact, he helps so much that when he's caught, he's charged with the same crime as the principal. In addition to helping the principal, the accomplice actually wants the crime to succeed, and acts accordingly.

An example of this is if you put on a ski mask and go with Roger to rob the bank. That's enough of an overt act (remember those?) that it doesn't really matter what else you do at the bank. You might not be an accomplice if you actually go with Roger with the intent of stopping him, or if you're secretly working for the cops. In those cases, you don't want Roger to succeed, so you don't have the intent to be an accomplice.

TAINTED LOVE: In 2004, "Juliet" was convicted of her part in the murders during a robbery at a Detroit convenience store. Her boyfriend, "Romeo," had been the principal, but police claimed that Juliet had acted as a lookout and even told Romeo when more people were entering the store. Juliet argued that she had no part in the killings and was only there because she was terrified of what Romeo would do if she didn't participate. The jury wasn't buying it, and Juliet now faces up to life in prison. As for Romeo, he shot and killed himself the night of the robbery.

Street Law Concept #62: Aiding and Abetting

Historically, aiding and abetting was considered its own crime, so you'd be charged not with robbery, but with "aiding and abetting" robbery. Aiding and abetting is a lesser offense, meaning you do less than if you were an accomplice.

So if you tell Roger the vault's combination and tell him that Saturday is the best day to rob the bank, you're guilty of aiding and abetting a robbery, even if you don't get a piece of the action. (Note: while technically aiding and abetting is a lesser offense, most states will treat you the same as if you were an accomplice.)

> **Street Law Concept #63: Co-conspirator**
> The co-conspirator agrees to do the crime with Roger and takes some action to prove that he's serious or to further the future crime.

You don't have to lift a finger to be guilty of conspiracy. All you have to do is agree to commit the crime with Roger, and do something that shows you're serious. So where's the harm? If a cop is listening in on your conversation and believes that you're serious, he can charge you with conspiracy—even if you never get to the bank.

> **Street Law Concept #64: Accessory After the Fact**
> The accessory after the fact had nothing to do with the crime, but either helps the criminals escape (or hides them) or somehow knowingly benefits from the crime. "Knowingly benefits" means that you knew the crime occurred, and you know that the benefits you're getting are from that crime.

You can be an accessory after the fact even if you didn't know Roger was planning to rob the bank. In fact, say you had nothing to do with the robbery—you found out about it a day later, when Roger hands you a gold watch that he stole from a security-deposit box. In accepting the stolen watch, and knowing it was from the bank robbery, you've become an accessory after the fact.

All these various categories show that it's easy to get busted for things your friends do—especially if you're (1) in the area when they do it, (2) get them supplies to do it, or (3) profit when they do it.

LIFE AIN'T THAT CHEAP: In August of 2000, "Madame Bovary" was in the middle of a divorce when it suddenly occurred to her that she might just look better as a widow. Smartly sharing her concerns with a stranger in a bar, she found herself eventually face-to-face with a hired killer who said he'd do it for $500. Madame Bovary forked over $100, but met with her friendly assassin later to say she'd changed her mind. Her killer turned out to be undercover detective "Flaubert," and Madame Bovary was promptly arrested. Strangely, she was charged with "wanton endangerment"—a charge usually used, for example, if you don't tell the person you're sleeping with that you're HIV-positive. Why didn't they charge her with conspiracy or solicitation? Because her change of mind would have been a valid defense to either of those charges, but not a "wanton endangerment" charge. Though Madame Bovary was originally convicted, a higher Kentucky court reversed it, saying that the particular elements of "wanton endangerment" hadn't been proven.

Generally speaking, the more of the three standards you meet, the more likely it is that cops will charge you for a crime. Simply being in the vicinity of a crime—a circle of pot smokers, graffiti artists writing on a wall—is generally not enough proof that you yourself were committing a crime. The best defense, of course, is to be nowhere near the pot smoking, the prank, or any other misconduct.

In most states, you are not required to report a crime, or evidence of a crime, if you don't want to. The exception is when you are being interrogated by the cops and refuse to cooperate. If the cops believe that you are hindering their investigation, they can charge you with obstruction.

Street Law Concept #65: Obstruction of Justice

This crime generally occurs when you interfere with the police or other law enforcement officials. It doesn't matter if a crime has actually been committed, or if the police are even in the middle of a formal investigation. (Although these two circumstances are the most likely to lead to an obstruction of justice charge.)

SNITCHES AND UNDERCOVER COPS

The enemy of every good buzz, score, or prank is the undercover cop—and his civilian buddy, the snitch.

Street Law Concept #66: Snitch/Informant

A snitch is a civilian (i.e., not a law enforcement official) who offers information regarding criminal activities—often for a reduced sentence or to escape punishment entirely for his crimes.

Sometimes snitches are friends who have a grudge against you. They can even be your co-conspirators, your partners in crime, your soon-to-be-ex-friends—who, to save their own asses, have made deals with the police to get the goods on you.

Undercover cops are another story. They're professionally trained to get your trust and gather information. The first urban myth of undercover cops is that if you ask her "Are you a cop?" then she has to tell you the truth. The other myth is that you can always spot a narc because he won't do drugs with you. Neither myth is true. An undercover cop doesn't have to tell you he's a cop, and narcs, in many circumstances, are allowed to do drugs so they don't blow their cover.

Say It Ain't So, Man!: Was Timothy Leary actually working for the man? It seems so. In 1999, the FBI released documents that show that Leary turned snitch after his arrest in 1974 for his 1971 prison break. The counterculture demigod claimed that he wanted a "collaborative relationship" with law enforcement and promptly started naming names of the very folks who helped him escape. But maybe he had something up his sleeve after all: a lot of the information was out-of-date and led to no arrests. Leary supporters claim that he was always open about being "forced" to co-operate to reduce his prison charge. At any rate, Leary, who died in 1996, won't be around to tell us the truth.

It's pretty hard for us civilians to spot an undercover cop or a snitch. A common trick by cops is the "babe" cop—that really hot chick who suddenly takes a liking to you and your activities. Babes can be cops, too.

ENTRAPMENT

The last desperate hope of scofflaws everywhere. I mean, the cop offered you drugs, didn't he? Doesn't that mean he entrapped you? What about a cop asking to buy drugs? What if a cop asks me to find him a prostitute? A stolen car? A rare painting? Isn't he tricking me?

Street Law Concept #67: Entrapment

A cop entraps you when he coerces/bribes/convinces you to commit a crime that you had absolutely no previous intent to commit. That last part is important—if any part of the crime was your idea initially, then you won't have an entrapment defense, even if the government provides you with the "ideal opportunity" to commit the crime.

Don't count on entrapment getting you out of trouble. It's hard to prove—mainly because cops are allowed to lie and to trick people all the time. You need all three of the following to prove a case of entrapment:

The Three Requirements for Entrapment

- Evidence shows that you would never have committed the crime without the cop's interference.
- The cop planned the whole crime herself—you had absolutely no part in the planning.
- The cop used either trickery or force—or some kind of persuasion or fraud.

You've got to show that you, as a person, would not have committed the crime if the cop hadn't done all of the above. Note that it's even harder to prove entrapment by a snitch!

So when can you prove entrapment? Standards vary from state to state, but generally, you might be entrapped if the cop does one or more of the following:

Possible Methods of Entrapment

- Unreasonably pressures you
- Threatens you or your family with bodily harm

- Promises that the police will never find out about your involvement
- Bribes you with exorbitant sums of money or another over-whelming incentive
- Works really hard to make you feel sorry for her situation
- Claims that someone will be hurt or killed if you don't commit the crime
- Manipulates you by imposing on your friendship/relationship with her

BUT IT WAS A NICE TRY, BUDDY: Arrested for possessing less than fifty grams of a controlled substance, "Don Quixote" had a great defense—he'd been entrapped by Michigan police. The court bought it and dismissed all charges related to a March 28, 2001, transaction. Unfortunately, Quixote was still under arrest. Why? Because of a second transaction he'd undertaken on April 2, 2001—with a different undercover cop, and no entrapment occurring. The court found that just because you've been entrapped the first time doesn't mean you get a defense to every other stupid, voluntary move you make afterward.

WARRANTS

"We have a warrant for your arrest!" Cops are always saying that. Sounds official, doesn't it? Actually, a warrant is just a piece of paper.

Street Law Concept #68: Warrant

A warrant is an official piece of paper that authorizes law enforcement officials to do something. Yeah, this isn't too specific. But it is usually granted by judges/magistrates, and cops have to apply for it.

Essentially, you need to know about two types of warrants:

Street Law Concept #69: Arrest Warrant

An arrest warrant authorizes a law enforcement official to arrest someone. The officer may also search the immediate area around the arrest for weapons. A cop usually needs a warrant to arrest you at your house.

In many situations, a cop does not need an arrest warrant, for example, if he thinks (1) you've just committed or are about to commit a crime, (2) other people are about to get hurt, (3) you're about to destroy evidence or property, or (4) there's already a warrant out for your arrest for another crime. If the arrest takes place in your house, the cop can check the house for other people and look around. For anything further, they usually need a search warrant. Usually.

Street Law Concept #70: Search Warrant

In most instances, a cop needs a search warrant to look for evidence in private property, or in public property not generally accessible to the public. The warrant must describe the place to be searched and describe what the police are looking for.

These descriptions set limits to the search. If the police are looking for a stolen car, they shouldn't be looking in your medicine cabinets without a really good reason. Most of the time, though, cops can check the area around your house, including backyards, toolsheds, attics, garbage cans, etc., on your property. They can usually search cars on the property, too. Cops can go beyond the search warrant if they think you're going to destroy evidence, or to find out more about the evidence that they already have. A bad search warrant can get the search—and everything found during the search—thrown out of court.

There are some general rules about warrants. They have to be "fresh"—no more than three to ten days old. Misdemeanor warrants usually have to be served during the daytime—say, from six A.M. to ten P.M. The cops doing the searching have to look like cops—no disguises allowed. If the cops don't have a search warrant, they may ask you to consent to a search—usually telling you that it'll be less trouble than making them come back with one.

GRENADES IN HARLEM: "Auntie Mame," a fifty-seven-year-old New Yorker, was in the wrong place at the wrong time . . . home. On May 16, 2003, armed cops kicked down the door to her apartment and threw a flash grenade in. The blinding light and noise, along with being handcuffed and yelled at, was too much for Mame; she died of cardiac arrest soon after. Even worse—the cops had the wrong apartment. Acting on a tip from an apparently incompetent snitch that cocaine and heroin were stored in the apartment, the cops had a special "no knock" warrant allowing them to break in without warning. When Auntie Mame became short of breath, the paramedics were summoned, but it was too late. While city officials apologized and lots of cops were "reassigned," both flash grenades and no-knock warrants are still used by the NYPD.

When a cop stops you on the street, he can check if any warrants are outstanding for your arrest. An outstanding arrest warrant just means that you're wanted by the cops, and there was enough evidence to arrest you for a previous crime. Cops will either call your name and address in—or, more likely, they'll have a computer in their car that will do it for them. An outstanding arrest warrant gets you arrested immediately, usually with no questions asked.

SEARCHES

Pay attention: thousands of cases and trials hinge on whether a search is legal. Millions of words have been written about what constitutes a search. Here's what you need to know. The Fourth Amendment of the Bill of Rights protects you against unlawful searches and seizures. Simple.

The main thing you should remember, though, is that cops need a search warrant when you have a reasonable expectation of privacy in the location you're in. You expect to have some privacy in your bedroom. You expect to have some privacy in your pants. There's no expectation of privacy in the front seat of your car when it's on the road. But when it's parked in your garage, you expect some privacy.

The other thing you should be aware of is consent. Cops prefer if you consent to a search, because getting a search warrant can be a pain in the ass. You don't have to consent—but it's best to withhold consent in a way that doesn't make the cops suspicious.

Street Law Concept #71: Consent

This is a pretty basic concept—you agree to do something. However, for your consent to be legal, you have to be physically capable of consenting (meaning you can communicate your consent so someone else can understand). You have to be legally allowed to consent, which rules out not only minors and the insane, but people who aren't authorized to give consent in the situation. And the consent has to be given freely—no threats or bullying involved.

Searches of You

When a cop goes through your pockets, it's obviously a search. But getting a hair sample, requiring a urine test, etc., are also searches of your person. A wiretap is a search. So is going through your e-mail. A cop needs a good reason—probable cause, usually—to get this stuff.

Without an arrest, a cop can search you, but only to a limited extent. Most detention searches have already been described—the right-to-inquire search, the reasonable-suspicion search. In a detention search, a cop can't go through your pockets without probable cause. She can, however, pat you down to make sure you're not carrying weapons. A hard bulge vaguely shaped like a weapon will make her suspicious. Generally, these searches don't require that you be moved to a different location.

Once you're arrested, searches get serious. In some cases, you might end up with the dreaded strip search. More on that in the next chapter.

BIG MAN ON CAMPUS?: If you find your teacher staring at your crotch, don't worry. She might just be looking for drugs. This is precisely what happened to a student at the Carl Sandburg High School in 1991. "Anne," a teacher's aide, notified the principal and teacher that student "Crusoe Robinson" was "a little too endowed in the crotch." (That's no crime! That's just good news!) The dean detained Crusoe Robinson and called "Mrs. Robinson," his mother, for permission to conduct a search. Mrs Robinson refused consent, but the dean proceeded anyway. Crusoe Robinson was told to take off his clothes in the school locker room—but no drugs were found. His outraged mother filed suit against the school district. Unfortunately for Crusoe, the court found that, given rumors of his drug dealing and "furtive behavior" when confronted, the school had a right to investigate in this manner. Which leaves open the question of what was more embarrassing—the search or Mommy's lawsuit.

Searches of Your Car

Bad news, folks—you have less of an expectation of privacy in your car than you do in your house. This is partly because cars require registration, but also because when you're driving a car, you're out in public, and you're mobile (which means you can get away easier). The worse you're driving, or the worse shape your car is in, the more likely that you'll be pulled over. And that has bigger consequences than you think.

Street Law Concept #72: Vehicle Exemption

A police officer who pulls a car over for any reason (a traffic violation, a bad taillight, swerving) has a right to search the car *if* he has probable cause that would get him a warrant, or a reasonable suspicion that you're doing something illegal. In these circumstances, he does not need a warrant to search the car.

Once the car is stopped, a cop can ask you for your license and registration. He can also ask you a few preliminary questions. In the most routine of stops, the cop will run a check on your license. That little card will give him your age, address, Social Security number, and a description of you. It will also tell him about any major traffic convictions in the last seven years, and if you've failed to appear in court. This is not the time, therefore, to bust out the fake ID and see if it works.

MENACE TO SOCIETY?: "Mother Goose" was driving her two kids to soccer practice when she was pulled over by the cops for not wearing her seat belt. What happened next is a matter of some dispute, but when Mother Goose stated that she couldn't produce identification because her purse had been stolen, "Officer Humpty" decided to handcuff her, arrest her, and haul her into jail. (A neighbor took her frightened kids home.) Mother Goose languished in jail on the seatbelt charge for hours before she was released on $310 bond. The fine for not wearing a seat belt in Austin, Texas? Fifty dollars. This case went all the way to the U.S. Supreme Court. In 2001, the justices admitted that Officer Humpty had acted with "extreme poor judgment" but nonetheless upheld Mother Goose's conviction, stating that Officer Humpty had not violated Mother Goose's constitutional rights by jailing her for a $50 offense.

What happens next is up to the cop's level of suspicion. Does he smell smoke? Are you acting shifty? A cop might ask you to step out of the car (he doesn't need a reason for that). He and his partner can separate you and your friends so you can be questioned separately.

He does, however, need probable cause to search your car more thoroughly. If he doesn't have one, he might ask for your consent to do so. Whether you consent is up to you. You have the right not to consent, but if the manner of your nonconsent makes him suspicious, he might detain you longer.

FOGGY WINDOWS AND CRACK COCAINE: A parked car with fogged-up windows can mean many things. It could be a nice night on Lovers' Lane, or cause for reasonable suspicion on the part of the local cops. Ohio cop "Huggy Bear" found his suspicions confirmed when he approached a parked car and found "Starsky" and "Hutch" highly intoxicated inside. A quick check revealed outstanding warrants, and both men were arrested—but not before Starsky consented to a search, which revealed a stash of crack. Starsky tried to contest the search later, stating that Huggy Bear didn't have enough for reasonable suspicion, but the court disagreed. The fact that the men had been sitting for a while parked in a car, in a high-crime neighborhood—and in freezing weather—was enough for the initial investigative stop. After that, the two men pretty much dug themselves in deeper with conflicting answers and apparent intoxication.

A probable cause search allows the cop to search for weapons and contraband. He can't open your trunk or your locked glove box. Basically, he's searching the seats and the floorboards for weapons that your passenger or you have access to. If he sees anything in plain view, he'll take it. Once he finds something in one of these places—a weapon, your stash, an illegal immigrant hiding in your backseat—then he gets to do a search incident to an arrest.

Street Law Concept #73: Search Incident to an Arrest

As previously stated, when a cop arrests you, he can search the area immediately around you for evidence, weapons, or contraband. What does this mean for your car? A cop can search the passenger compartment more thoroughly and open unsealed packages or unlocked containers. The search must take place at approximately the same time as the arrest.

Once you're arrested, your car will be impounded, and the cops will do a more thorough search at the impound lot.

Searches of Your House

The rules about home searches vary, but there are ten basic concepts to keep in mind.

10 Rules About Home Searches

1. You do not have to be home when the cops arrive to search.
2. Cops do not need a warrant to search your garbage when it's on the street. They do need one when it's in your backyard.
3. Cops without a warrant will try to get you to consent to a search. Never sign the consent form. Always ask for a warrant. The cop might ignore you, but at least it's clear that you didn't consent.
4. You do not have to open the door if the cops don't have a warrant. Once the door is open, a cop can say he hears something strange or smells something funny. From there it's only a few steps to probable cause . . .
5. After the police leave, take pictures before you clean. See if anything is missing.
6. If they only have an arrest warrant, walk outside, close the door behind you, and lock it. They should need a separate search warrant for the house.
7. Someone who "apparently" has authority can consent to a search. This includes roommates. However, roommates cannot give permission to search your room.
8. Even without a search warrant, a cop can confiscate something in plain view.
9. Always read the warrant to make sure it's timely, to see what they're looking for and where they're allowed to look.
10. Even with a search warrant for the house, a cop isn't supposed to search people in the house without a separate warrant. Technically, therefore, they shouldn't be searching you when you're visiting a friend's house. There are exceptions.

Once again, a person does not have to consent to a search, and the cops should not bully him into doing so. It is quite possible to request that the police return at a more suitable or more convenient time, or when they have a search warrant. Some cops might perform a search anyway, disregarding your lack of consent.

RAID AT THE USHERS': When Bureau of Alcohol, Tobacco, and Firearms agent "Poe" got a tip that the "Ushers" possessed weapons such as a rocket launcher and grenades, he quickly made up a search warrant. Too quickly, in fact—he forgot to state what exactly the agents expected to find at the Ushers' home. The warrant was issued, and the house was searched, but no illegal weapons were found. The Ushers sued Poe and the department for an illegal search and violation of their constitutional rights. The case went all the way to the U.S. Supreme Court, which stated, in a 5–4 decision, that Poe should've been more careful filling out that search warrant. Since he wasn't, he could be sued in civil court just like anyone else.

Miscellaneous Searches

Search law has many gray areas. For example, if you're still in school, what about your locker? And if you're an adult, what about that locker you rent from the gym? Can the cops search your office? What about your hotel room? The answer to all these questions is . . . well, it depends.

In the past, a hotel clerk couldn't give permission for a search of a guest's room, but that now varies from state to state. School locker searches can occur if school officials have a "reasonable suspicion" that a school ordinance has been violated. This is a more lenient standard than for adults because authorities must weigh the protections of the Constitution against the standards of safety for other students. The standards of searches in offices and other semipublic places are also complicated. For example, in New York, the police need a warrant to search your office, but health officials do not. It's best to generally assume you have less privacy once you leave the house.

> **BIG BANG BABY:** Nobody likes to change diapers, not even a state trooper. But sometimes it's part of the job description. "Daddy" was pulled over for speeding by "Trooper," in northwest Indiana. When Trooper called Daddy's info in, he discovered that Daddy was a suspect in a drug investigation. Trooper asked Daddy to step out of the car, and as he did, Trooper noticed that "Baby's" diaper seemed unusually heavy. Trooper searched Baby and found approximately $145,000 worth of cocaine. A search with drug dogs also revealed that "Mommy" had two stashes of weed in her socks. Both parents were charged with possession with intent to distribute, but Daddy claimed that the search of Baby was unconstitutional. Stay tuned . . .

Consent

As you can see, consent is a really important issue. Whether you consent to a search is up to you. Technically, cops should not arrest you simply because you don't consent to a search of your person, your house, or your car. But yelling "No—don't go in there!" is pretty damn unlikely to help you. You have every right to refuse consent, but if you do it in a nice, friendly, calm way—maybe even with a plausible excuse for why not—you should be left alone.

The worst thing a person can do is to be unclear about his/her lack of consent. Saying what you'd wish, you'd like, or phrasing your lack of consent as a question will confuse the cops and make your case much more difficult in court. Note that consent is often accompanied by actions. Looking uncertain but opening the door wider sends the cops two differing messages. Whatever decision you make, be clear and firm.

Some cops will search anyway. Keep your eyes open and tell your lawyer later.

> **THIS IS NOT SMART:** Cops came to the house of "Robin Hood" in 2003 looking for a couple of fugitives who were rumored to be hiding at that address. Robin was happy to cooperate, since he knew nothing about that, and consented to a warrantless search of everywhere "but the garage." Which made the cops say—huh? Their suspicions aroused, they went back to get a search warrant and found the remains of a meth lab. Mr. Hood, the good, but not particularly bright, citizen, was promptly arrested.

THEY'RE GONNA FIND IT!

The cop is hovering over a stash box. It's closed, but inside is a substantial amount of weed, and the dealer's number. He doesn't seem overly suspicious, but he's looking at it with some curiosity. Horrified, you can hear him saying the words . . .

"What's that?"

What do you do? The instinct is to deny everything. "What's what? That? It's not mine. I have no idea! I didn't know it was there!" This is both good and bad. While the instinct is to deny all knowledge and appear as blank as possible, there is always the question of standing.

> **Street Law Concept #74: Standing**
>
> A person needs standing to initiate any kind of lawsuit. You also need standing to protest an action by cops, DAs, or judges. Standing means that you are directly affected by a particular action, and that the law has provided a remedy for whatever the conflict is.

For example, you can't start a lawsuit against Dunkin' Donuts just because they fired your friend. That's your friend's problem, so what's it to you? Similarly, you can't file a complaint with the cops that your friend's boyfriend stole her earrings. She has to do that herself.

So, if you say the box isn't yours, you have no rights that were violated when the cop opens it without your consent. It wasn't your box, remember? Claiming it's yours now, after the cops find your stash, is obviously a bad idea. Once you deny the stash box is yours, you forfeit all right to protest a search.

What you actually say to the cop is up to you. Some people avoid answering questions and like to be as vague as possible. Others might deny the box is theirs and lose standing if the box is opened. Another might state that he can't open it because it doesn't belong to him. The cop might just leave. Some adventurous types try to distract the cops by responding to questions with questions. These tactics may work in some situations and fail in others. (As a general rule, flattery and bribery both fail. Don't try either.) Cops may or may not open the package. It matters what the package is. For example, cops aren't always keen on opening someone's stamped, addressed package because federal law actually governs the mail. But it all depends on their suspicions, their mood, your behavior, and about twenty other factors.

An informal poll shows some of the possible responses to "What's that?" Note that these responses haven't been field-tested and are therefore definitely not guaranteed.

Possible Responses to "What's That?"
1. Something I'm delivering for a friend.
2. It's a present from my cheating ex-boyfriend, the jerk.
3. I found it somewhere.
4. I was just going to throw that away!
5. God, I can't keep track of the stuff in here!

A CONTROVERSIAL SOLUTION

The Apology.

That's right. For minor infractions—jaywalking, making a racket in public, littering, trespassing in a park after hours—the Apology could work magic. A cop, after all, doesn't want to spend his night writing up citations for every well-intentioned mistake he sees. A sheepish smile and an apologetic statement—"I'm really, really sorry. I won't do it again"—may induce the police officer to let you go with a verbal warning.

> **DIRTY, DIRTY HARRY:** Meet Officer "Humbert" and his liberated views of crime and punishment. Upon discovering a teenage couple making out in a car, Humbert threatened to arrest them for lewd conduct. When the couple pleaded with him, he allowed them to evade the arrest if each did topless jumping jacks and push-ups for his viewing pleasure. The teenagers

complied, but told their folks the next day. Humbert declined to take a lie detector test and resigned quickly before he was terminated. He is the subject of an ongoing criminal investigation.

You will not find the Apology in law books. It is far from guaranteed and certainly not recommended in every case. For example, the Apology will almost never work when you are caught with drugs. It may—possibly, in rare circumstances—work if you're busted with a small amount of weed. A busy, distracted, or liberal-minded cop might just confiscate the pot and let you go. Anything heavier, or in greater amounts, it's best to keep quiet and refuse to answer any questions.

The Thirteen Golden Rules of Dealing with the Police

1. Stay calm.
2. Do not answer any questions relating to the incident—unless you really want to help them solve the crime.
3. Keep your hands visible.
4. Never touch the officer.
5. Ask if you are free to go.
6. Be polite and pleasant when you have to talk.
7. Look at the officer's badge for his badge number and name.
8. Note the time of day.
9. Listen for what you're being charged with, if anything.
10. Stay in a public location. Do not agree to move to another location.
11. Neither confirm nor deny ownership of suspicious items.
12. Remember that you do not have to consent to a search.
13. Be alert to witnesses and observers.

CONCLUSION

How you're treated by cops depends a lot on how you treat them. But sometimes, nothing you say is going to change a cop's mind about what a lowlife you are. As stated earlier, you never know the personality of the cop you're dealing with. If it appears the cop isn't willing to negotiate, then keep reading; there's advice on how to survive the arrest and the jail time.

CHAPTER 5

Worst-Case Scenario: Go Directly to Jail

INTRODUCTION

Hey, you're only human. You tried everything to stay out of trouble. But somehow, for some reason, it went wrong. Now there's a cop standing in front of you with the unmistakable look in his eye that says, "Buddy, you're comin' in." Welcome to the world of arrest, jail, and court.

Sure, you might never need this section. But just in case . . . now is not the time to cry for mommy. Now is the time to keep your wits about you. Bear in mind that the information and advice in this chapter come informally from a variety of sources, from public defenders to police officers to legal texts. In some cases it will keep your undignified encounter with the law from becoming the worst thing in your life.

First, the general rules when things get serious:

The Three Rules of Being Arrested

1. Do not panic.
2. Be polite: do not aggravate the man with the gun.
3. Say only this: "I am going to be silent. I want a lawyer."

Number 3 is extremely important. Whether you did what you were accused of or not, your best bet is to keep silent until you speak to a lawyer who can advise you about your options and your rights. (Remember, even if you're caught red-handed, you still have legal rights.) Your right to be silent does have limitations. You are generally expected to answer when they ask you for your name and address. But otherwise, whenever anyone asks you a question, you do have the option to be silent. A cop is, technically, supposed to stop asking you questions when you state that you want to be silent. But be aware that not all cops will stop asking questions.

ARE YOU REALLY GOIN' IN?

There is some good news. In some states, a cop might not bother with a full arrest for nonviolent misdemeanors. He can just write you a citation that requires you to show up in court for an arraignment.

Street Law Concept #75: Citation

This is a written mandate that states that you are required to appear in a court of law. If you can't show up, you need to have a damn good explanation, which you must get approved by a judge.

Street Law Concept #76: Arraignment

This is generally the first hearing when you're accused of a crime. At this stage, you're formally charged with the offense, and you enter your plea. If you don't have to enter your plea, then it's usually called a *presentment*.

In some states, for some crimes, the citation-and-release is mandatory. In other areas, it's up to the cop's discretion. In other states, it's not an option. Getting a citation is a lot easier than being arrested and booked at a police station. You can ask the officer, in a nonthreatening way, if this is possible.

KING OF THE SLIP: In some cases, if you're rich, famous, or both, you won't have the cops knocking on your door. Instead, your lawyer will politely be informed that a warrant has been issued for your arrest. Witness the arrest of Michael Jackson for child-molestation charges. Jackson was in Vegas when the California warrant was issued. Spared the mess of the local sheriff and deputies kicking down his door, Jackson was allowed to surrender to authorities. (He was slapped with cuffs, though.) After putting up $3 million in bail, Jackson then retreated back to Vegas. Which is curious, since, most of the time, you're not supposed to leave the state you've been arrested in . . . but maybe the court felt that Jackson wouldn't be a flight risk. After all—where was he going to go that he wouldn't be recognized?

If you're drunk, however, it's off to the drunk tank. Known formerly as protective custody, this is where you'll stay until you sober up. Unless you were drunkenly assaulting someone, you might just be able to go home . . . with a citation. Again, it depends on where you are.

Take that citation seriously. If you don't show up at your arraignment, the judge will swear out a warrant for your arrest. The cops will either start looking for you or just wait until they see you the next time. Either way, you'll be in the cuffs before you can open your mouth.

MIRANDA MYTHS

Every cop on television starts reciting the Miranda warnings as if he were reciting a speech in front of a school assembly. You know the drill: you have the right to remain silent, blah blah blah. How many times have you seen a fictional perp get off because he wasn't "Mirandized" properly? Gives you hope, doesn't it?

Don't jump to conclusions. First things first—what is Miranda?

Street Law Concept #77: Miranda Warnings
These warnings are connected to your right against self-incrimination, and your right to have legal counsel before a custodial interrogation. What does all this mean? Keep reading . . .

A BRIEF HISTORY: Americans have Ernesto Miranda to thank for their Miranda rights. (Not that they did him any good.) Ernesto was picked up for stealing $8 and—caught without his copy of *The Street Law Handbook*—ended up confessing not only to the theft, but also to the kidnapping and rape of an eighteen-year-old woman. In 1966, the Supreme Court overturned his conviction and decided that all suspects must be given what are now known as Miranda warnings prior to questioning. Unfortunately for Ernesto, he was retried for the rape, convicted, and served fourteen years before being paroled—only to die later in a knife fight.

All cops have to recite the Miranda warnings when they begin to interrogate someone in custody. In case you haven't been watching your *Law & Order,* here's what the warnings should sound like. They might not sound exactly like this, but they should be damn close.

Miranda Warnings

1. You have the right to remain silent.
2. Anything you say can and will be used against you in a court of law.
3. You have the right to have an attorney present before any questioning.
4. If you cannot afford an attorney, one will be appointed to represent you before any questioning. Do you understand these rights?

If you are taken into custody and not given this rundown, then the cops have acted improperly. Your case could be thrown out. But don't jump to conclusions. Miranda only applies when *all three* of the following are present:

1. you are being interrogated;
2. you are being interrogated by a police officer, or another law enforcement official; and
3. you are in custody or reasonably believe that you are in custody.

Street Law Concept #78: Custody

You are in custody when you, as a reasonable person, do not feel free to leave the situation. You are either being physically restrained (cuffs, etc.) or told by an authority that you are not free to leave.

What does this mean? It means that cops can ask you to come in to speak with them, but if you know you're free to leave, you're not in custody and you won't get Miranda warnings. It means if you voluntarily say anything (i.e., you were not asked a question, coaxed, or intimidated by the cops), then the *Miranda* warnings are not necessary. This includes instances where you said you were going to be silent and the cops left you alone—but you started babbling anyway. This does not include instances where you said you were silent, but the cops kept asking questions. Your best bet? Do not volunteer a statement, ever. A voluntary statement is not protected by Miranda, since the cops need to be actually interrogating you for Miranda to apply.

Here's a question: Shouldn't you start hearing Miranda warnings the minute you're arrested? Not necessarily. Remember, Miranda only applies if you're being interrogated *and* are in custody. *Both*. So if a couple of quiet cops slap the cuffs on you and don't ask questions—no Miranda. And if the reverse—lots of questions, but you're on a street corner, no cuffs in sight, free to walk away—ditto. No Miranda.

BRAGGING IS NOT A GOOD IDEA: When the cops tell you that any statement you make "can be used against you in court," pay attention—it's not just lip service. During his trial, teenage sniper suspect Lee Boyd Malvo was faced with his own damning statements made during police interrogation. Malvo, perhaps unwisely, bragged about his marksmanship skills, his teamwork with fellow sniper John Allen Muhammad, and even laughed as he recalled how he shot some of his victims dead. Cops promptly played the recorded statements to the trial jury. Considering Muhammad was sentenced to death, Malvo might be regretting his exercise in free speech.

Say you're arrested, interrogated, and you end up confessing to the whole thing. You never once heard your Miranda warnings, which triggers your *Street Law Handbook* radar. You tell your lawyer, and you get off scot-free, right? Wrong again. Your arrest remains legal. It's all your self-incriminating statements that get thrown out.

Street Law Concept #79: Self-Incrimination

Just remember, the purpose of the Miranda warnings is to protect you against self-incrimination. This comes from the Fifth Amendment, which also protects you against self-incrimination in court. Note that neither the Miranda warnings or the Fifth Amendment will protect you against voluntary statements or information unrelated to criminal charges.

The cops now have the job of presenting the DA with a case, but without the help of your incriminating statements. Rest assured, now that they know you did it, they'll be nosing around for other evidence against you. You might walk, you might not, depending on what evidence is out there, and how good your lawyer is at dealing with it.

Street Law Concept #80: Evidence

Just a primer on a complicated topic: evidence includes testimony of witnesses, your testimony, records and other material, physical evidence, or anything that relates to the fact-gathering—and ultimate truth—of the case.

Also, you probably won't get a Miranda warning if there's an outstanding warrant for your arrest for another charge. The cops who pick you up the second time don't need to—you've already heard your rights. Right?

To give you more detail, let's look at interrogation and custody again.

INTERROGATION

Forget about sitting in a dark room at the police station with someone shining a bright white light in your face. The first thing you should know is that an interrogation can happen anywhere, and that the sole purpose of an interrogation is to get information from you. The cops are not trying to be friendly, no matter how cool they may seem.

Street Law Concept #81: Interrogation

This is a term for when the police question suspects and witnesses about a particular crime or incident. Interrogation does not have to be a formal proceeding; it is primarily a fact-gathering mission for the police.

Second, a cop is allowed to lie. That's right. They're not allowed to lie about everything, but they are allowed to twist the truth, to make conversation, and to lead you astray. Remember, they're not trying to get to know you. This is their job. Here are some common police interrogation techniques.

Common Cop Techniques

- **Good Cop/Bad Cop**. While you're being yelled at by Bad Cop, the other cop comes in and pulls him off. You think Good Cop is your friend, so you're ready to open up. The oldest trick in the book. But when you're being interrogated, nobody is your friend—except your lawyer.

- **Everybody's doin' it**. People like to stick together. If the cop tells you that your friends are squealing—and, incidentally, cutting better deals for themselves—you might be tempted, too. Before you give in to temptation, remember—a cop can say he knows things that he doesn't know for a fact and say your friends are saying things that they're not saying.

- **Honesty is the best policy**. The cop tells you that if you confess, the judge will go easy on you. This may be true for your parents, but the judge is not your dad. This is not how the law works. Talk to your lawyer before you "make it easy on yourself."

- **Share with me, sweetheart**. The cops are not out to get you. They just want information. You're not even a suspect—just help 'em to figure out what happened, and they'll let you go home. Except if you say anything incriminating, they'll slap the cuffs on you anyway. Again—not fair, not nice, but certainly not illegal.

- **Big bad cop**. She doesn't like your kind. She knows you're guilty. She's threatening to charge you with obstruction, with resisting arrest, if you don't answer her questions. Hell, she's looking forward to sending you to jail! Without actually intimidating you, she's prophesying all sorts of nasty stuff—all of which you can avoid if you do what she asks. Oh, brother. Remember, the DA charges you, not the cop.

- **Mr. Forgetful**. He asks you the question. Once. Twice. Then, twenty minutes later, he asks you again. Is he feeble? Hardly. If your story is phony, then you'll forget the details and eventually screw up.

In many cases, a cop will try to separate you from your friends to engage in one of the above maneuvers. There's little you can do about this. Keep your cool, and wait to talk to someone you know you can trust.

In case you start talking, remember this—you can

always again invoke your right to remain silent and shut up.

CUSTODY AND ARREST

If a cop feels that he has enough to bring you into custody, not much is going to change his mind. Tears, if they haven't already worked, will not work now. Excuses of the "I only inhaled once" variety will not impress him. He will not lighten up just because you suggest he should. And please don't try to bribe him. Not every cop can be bought off with $20, and that's just another charge that can be brought in against you. Once a cop has decided that he's going to go through the whole process of arresting and booking you, he's made his mind up.

Street Law Concept #82: Arrest

Technically, arrest means that you are deprived of your freedom by a law enforcement authority. However, you can also be under civilian arrest by a non-cop. An arrest means that you are facing the accusation that you have committed a crime.

Being arrested is a pain in the ass, but some things can make your arrest even worse.

Reasonable Force and Resisting Arrest

You might think you know what resisting arrest is: flailing your arms, hitting the cop, and shouting, "No, I won't go in, you pig!" However, there's a little more to it than that. A cop will use force if he reasonably feels that you are going to give him trouble. For example, if a cop gives a direct order—"leave this area at once"—and you refuse, that can be construed as a failure to comply, which can get you arrested. Even jostling the cop or giving him attitude can get you thrown in the back of the cop car.

THE MAN, THE MYTH, THE LEGEND: You know you're a big deal when Al Pacino plays you on the big screen. In the 1970s, Frank Serpico was an honest cop in an NYPD filled with corrupt ones. Over the course of his twelve-year career, Serpico repeatedly turned down bribes, turned in corrupt officers, and unsuccessfully tried to draw attention to the widespread corruption. Serpico retired in February of 1971 on a disability pension after being shot in the face by a dope pusher. (Many felt that the shooting was set up, since no cops called an "officer down" alert.) Later that year, Serpico's anti-corruption efforts were rewarded when the Knapp Commission convened and heard his testimony, which received national attention and a book deal. He became an even bigger celebrity after Pacino's portrayal of him in the movie *Serpico*. Decades later, in 1997, Serpico lashed out at the NYPD once again, stating that the problem with corrupt police started with America's weak leaders and poor role models. The police, he stated, just didn't know how to fight corruption in their own ranks—and there wasn't enough incentive to be a good cop.

Rest assured that the cops have a wide variety of methods to get you under control. If you're doubtful, take a good look at a police officer's uniform. The belt he wears weighs about twenty pounds with tools designed to be used for his protection, or to subdue unruly suspects.

Cop Methods for Dealing with Difficult Suspects

- **The "no weapons" method**. Cops can twist your wrists back and forth or bend your fingers backward. There are also a variety of choke holds (with or without props). If you've gone limp, they can drop you on your head or just drag you along.

- **Chemicals**. Pepper spray, Mace, and tear gas are all part of the cop's arsenal. So are flash grenades—when thrown, they'll blind you long enough for a cop to subdue you. Pepper spray is the most common—but be advised, this isn't the stuff you sprinkle in your soup. On rare occasions, it can blind or even kill you.

- **The hard stuff.** Cops can resort to their nightstick or a heavy flashlight. (These flashlights have up to six batteries, which can really, really hurt.) Cops also have blackjacks in stiff leather. Many would be happy to just use their fists.

- **Electricity.** No, this isn't a joke. In addition to stun guns, cops can use Tasers (which are basically stun guns that fire from a distance).

- **Backup.** When one cop just won't do, her friends will show up to show you the true meaning of compliance.

A cop is not supposed to use force disproportionate to the threat. That means if you're about to spit on him, and he coldcocks you, that should be illegal, right? Wrong. Cases like Amadou Diallo and Rodney King are rare, but courts often uphold arrests like these. Which means you can argue that he used excessive force—just don't be surprised if the judge throws your claim out of court.

To avoid misunderstandings—and violence—you should never, ever, touch an officer or any part of his uniform. You should also keep your hands in plain view, so he doesn't get nervous and freak out.

Chart 17: Penalties for Resisting Arrest

The following punishments are for resisting arrest by a law enforcement officer. Note that some states have differing penalties for resisting arrest in a nonviolent way, and resisting arrest with violence. The last thing you want is for this charge to escalate to assaulting a police officer, so always be careful.

City	Maximum Fine	Maximum Jail Time
Los Angeles	$1,000	1 year
District of Columbia	$5,000	5 years
Miami	$500	2 months
Chicago	$2,500	1 year (mandatory 48–100 hours of community service)
Las Vegas	$2,000	1 year
New York	$1,000	1 year
Dallas	$4,000	1 year

The Actual Arrest

The cop has already checked for outstanding warrants on you. In many states, he'll put in a call to whichever DA is currently doing "intake." He'll tell the DA the details of his probable cause, and the DA will give him the okay for the arrest and what you should be charged with. For emergency situations, really minor offenses, and other exceptions, the cop might not bother calling the DA.

Street Law Concept #83: Intake

An intake is one of the assistant DA's duties. When she is "on call," cops will be transferred to her to figure out whether they should charge a suspect and with what.

The cop will now probably pull your wrists behind your back and slap the cuffs on you. If he doesn't like you, he'll make them really tight. Then, as you're cuffed, he'll do a search—patting you down, going through your pockets, opening your bags. He might ask you questions as he searches. Remember your right to be silent, and listen for your Miranda rights. Try to remember when they were given to you. His partner—if he arrived in a patrol car—will also be watching and will call the station to say they're bringing a perp in. Most likely you'll be driven to the police station immediately. Pretty much all your requests now—bathroom, hunger, thirst, a change of channel on the radio—will be ignored.

At the station, you'll be at the front desk with your arresting officer(s). He will fill out a form with your name, address, and what the charge is. If you don't have an address, he'll ask you where you get your mail, and that's what he'll put down. Police stations can get hectic, or they can be deathly quiet, and either way, cops don't want you talking to other suspects in custody.

NICE TRY, SLICK: Some people will do anything to make their arrest go away. But flushing it down the toilet? That's what "Socrates," an inmate at Florida's St. Lucie County jail, tried to do. Arrested for armed robbery, the enterprising Socrates somehow got ahold of his arrest records and began flushing them down the jail toilet.

Unfortunately, the frequent flushing alerted authorities, who found pieces of paper floating in the bowl. Socrates apologized, and officials just typed up a new affidavit, leaving the old one for the plumber to deal with.

The cop will now conduct a more thorough search of your person. He should wear rubber gloves for this. He'll ask you whether you do drugs to see if you're coherent. He'll also ask you if you're sick and whether you have hepatitis, AIDS, or another disease to protect himself against your nasty germs. Always answer health questions, since they're for your own good—especially if you need medication later.

The cop will remove all your personal belongings from your person. You'll also have to give up everything that has a string—shoelaces, necklaces, the cord holding your sweatpants up. If he can't get them out, he'll cut them. In cases of drug possession, he might do a light massaging of your genitals, which may be beyond your control. The crotch is a popular place to hide drugs. Just make sure he (or she) is wearing gloves.

Your possessions will be marked and cataloged and set aside. If you go to jail, they'll be transported with you, but you won't see them again until your release. You can ask the officer what the procedure will be to retrieve your belongings. You might need a voucher. But remember, if the police confiscate possessions as evidence, you won't get them back.

Booking and Processing

- **Fingerprinting**. Most urban police stations have a fingerprinting machine that hooks up to an online directory. It works like a copy machine and you won't be able to trick it. Some states do palm printing as well.

- **Photograph**. Mug shots are accessible to the public. At the 2003 Oscars, Steve Martin showed the world Nick Nolte's mug shot—not flattering, since Nolte had been wandering around the desert high on mescaline for days.
- **Description**. The cop will enter you into the system. Relevant data include height, weight, hair color, race, skin color, tattoos and scars, age, etc. The system connects online.
- **Other samples**. Hair, skin, or blood samples generally require a warrant. You'll probably have to give these for the heavier crimes—rape or murder, for example.

The Dreaded Strip Search

Though it doesn't happen every time, some unfortunate souls will be subjected to the strip search. Certain crimes—resisting arrest, drug crimes, violent offenses—trigger the strip search more often. While the cops don't automatically have the right to strip-search you, they do have pretty broad discretion in this matter. It will be one of the more humiliating experiences in your life.

The first thing you should look for is a strip search from a same-sex officer. Another officer may be cataloging the search, but there shouldn't be anyone else there. Voyeurism is not a police privilege—certainly not by the opposite sex.

STRIP SEARCH, TEXAS STYLE: "Falstaff," an inmate in Texas, recently filed an unusual suit—to keep the female guards' hands off his birthday suit. Falstaff alleged a violation of his Fourth Amendment right against forcible search and seizure because male prisoners in the Estelle Unit, where Falstaff was incarcerated, were often strip-searched by female guards. Far from launching any prison fantasies, Falstaff stated the searches promoted "acts of misconduct" by the female guards as well as "open stares" and nasty comments. The courts agreed to hear this issue, given that strip searches by guards of the opposite gender were only supposed to occur in "extraordinary circumstances." However, charges against individual guards were soon dismissed.

Unfortunately, at this point, you will remove all your clothes. Then, you well bend over and be asked to spread your butt cheeks. Men might be asked to lift up their genitals to show the area under their scrotum. In particularly heinous cases, you might be subject to a body-cavity search. Your orifices—anus, vagina, etc.—will be manually probed for contraband. This should all be pretty private. However, in emergency situations, a cop can do all this searching *in the field*. Ouch!

OUCH, AGAIN: So he was carrying drugs. He deserved the arrest, right? Well, when undercover NYPD officers arrested alleged drug seller "Voltaire," for criminal sale and possession of a controlled substance, the courts got really interested . . . and not in a good way. You see, when the cops caught up to him, Voltaire was told to put his head through the rear window of the car and was then strip-searched—on a public street, in front of a crowd. Sure, the search led to two vials of heroin, but the courts threw out the charges, stating that a strip search in public should only occur in the most extreme of circumstances. The court found that it didn't matter that Voltaire's body cavities weren't searched—the strip search itself was violation enough.

Malicious or False Arrest

Though you should be keeping your mouth shut, this might be the time to start thinking about whether you're the victim of either malicious arrest or false arrest. It's been known to happen, and though neither charge is easy to prove, it's something to think about while you wait for your hearing—and your lawyer.

Street Law Concept #84: Malicious Arrest

Occurs when the cops arrest you without any probable cause, or while knowing that you didn't do the crime you were arrested for. This is hard to prove because you have to show that the cop actually knew you were innocent.

Street Law Concept #85: False Arrest

Is just an unlawful physical arrest or detention of yourself. Maybe they thought you were someone else, or they didn't bother calling the DA on intake. Maybe they intentionally "lost" your paperwork and kept you at the precinct. This, too, is difficult to prove.

The main goal of a malicious or false arrest charge against the cops is to show that they simply weren't doing their jobs. You can run the idea by your lawyer, but remember: these are legal terms, not your way of getting revenge at the guys who grabbed you. Cops get significant leeway in their arrests (they're trying to catch criminals, after all), so don't push for the charge unless your lawyer says you can back it up with the evidence.

Your Phone Call

"When do I get my phone call?" you demand righteously. Some bad news here—nothing in the Bill of Rights, the Constitution, the Declaration of Independence, or the Magna Carta entitles you to a phone call. That's right. The cops are not obliged by law to get you to a phone. The right to a phone call derives from your right to counsel. You are entitled to talk to a lawyer—and if you need a phone for that, you'll get one.

Once at the phone, you can call whomever you want. If you don't have your lawyer's number handy, try to get a friend or a parent on the phone to get one for you. However, do not, under any circumstances, assume that your phone call is private. Many courts have decided that you have no right to privacy regarding phone calls from jail or the precinct. You need to be careful about what you're saying, so don't take any chances. Stick to where you are, what you got arrested for, and what you need from your callee.

You are entitled to talk to a lawyer in a "reasonable" amount of time. That means your phone call can take place anywhere around twenty-four hours after your arrest. Take note of the time and just keep asking in a persistent, yet polite, way.

Bail Already?

In some states, you might talk to a pretrial officer before you head to jail. This person is here to help you get a cheap bond that will allow you to go free on your own recognizance. If the prospect of jail sounds unappealing, then by all means talk to her.

> **Street Law Concept #86: Bail**
>
> Bail is the court's way of letting you out of jail while guaranteeing that you will show up for all court hearings, and the trial—if there is one. Generally bail is money or some security that you must put up in order to walk now, appear in court later. The amount depends on your crime, your ability to pay, and the risk of your flight. It varies from state to state, but usually you have to put up 10 percent of the bail. You forfeit the whole bail if you run.

She should be asking basic questions—your name, address, personal references, your job and how long you've had it, etc. She's trying to see if you have strong enough ties to the community. She should not be asking you for any details about why you're here or what you were doing to get arrested. As friendly as she may seem, do not forget that she is an officer of the court. Pretend that the DA is in the room with you.

> **Street Law Concept #87: Bail Bondsperson**
>
> Bail bondspeople are in the business of helping you get bail. The bail bondsperson will usually write up a bond that the court will accept, allowing you to go free. You then owe the bail bondsperson the money, plus a fee.

If you qualify for one of these bonds, you'll pay a fee and go home, with a requirement that you appear in court again. If you don't, then it's off to jail.

NEVER ENOUGH: When alleged murderer "Byron" was brought before the court in Clark County, Washington, the judge set the bail at $150,000—not nearly enough according to victim "Shelley's" parents. However, Byron was dragged back into court when the cops discovered that the murder charges—as well as his consumption of alcohol and some cocaine—were violations of his parole from an earlier charge. The judge promptly placed Byron on a "no-bail hold," which means that he won't be getting out of jail until he's proven not guilty.

GO DIRECTLY TO JAIL, DO NOT PASS GO

There's no telling how long you'll be at the precinct. They might bundle you off to the jail immediately or just put you in a holding cell for a while. Remember, you are entitled to be before a judge within forty-eight hours of your arrest. It may be less, and it may be slightly more, but that's the guideline. Usually you'll travel by bus to the county jail, along with whatever other miscreants they picked up throughout the night.

While it might appear that you and your fellow prisoners are in the same boat (so to speak), they are not your friends. Even if they appear friendly sometimes, remember that most would be happy to cut a deal for a lighter sentence by ratting on you.

Jailhouse Procedures

Just like snowflakes, no two jails are alike. But they do all have one thing in common: they are rarely designed for your comfort. Here's a guide to Lockdown 101.

Your Guide to Jail

- **Attire.** You'll slip into a highly unattractive prison jumpsuit, which, regardless of your figure, will not flatter you.

- **Food.** Snacks, maybe. Around this time, you might be fed. The term *fed* must be interpreted loosely, as it might just be a dry sandwich in a paper bag.
- **Cell.** Overbooked. You will be packed into a cell full of same-sex prisoners, with alleged crimes ranging from murder to disorderly conduct. The really dangerous folk who can't control themselves will be off on their own.
- **Toilet.** It might be in a stall, it might not. It will be smack-dab in the middle of the cell, so if you're the delicate type who needs complete privacy to do your business, forget about it.
- **Sleep.** Little, if any. It's too crowded, too uncomfortable, and you'll be too nervous. There probably won't be room, anyway.
- **Visitors?** Not allowed.
- **Guards.** Are not your friends. Guards in jails have heard every story imaginable, and they're not interested in hearing yours. However, if you are polite and respectful, they might be accommodating if you have a serious request.

What If There's Trouble?

What if someone decides to get real friendly with you? Or unfriendly?

I WOULD'VE THOUGHT THEY VOTED INDEPENDENT!: In January of 2001, "Alexander Hamilton" was watching television with his fellow inmates in the Leon County, Florida, jail, when he just had to share his happiness that George W. Bush was on his way to the Oval Office. Hamilton probably thought he was safe, since most prisoners are registered Republicans. However, fellow inmate "Aaron Burr"—obviously a Democrat—was extremely offended by the Dubya praise and attacked Hamilton with a body slam. Burr was disciplined by prison officials.

First, don't panic. Remember, jail and prison are two different things.

Street Law Concept #88: Jail vs. Prison

Jail is generally the first step for anyone who is arrested. Prison usually follows when you've been convicted of a crime that results in a prison term. For example, Hugh Grant went to jail, while Robert Downey Jr. went to prison. Prison is much worse.

What does this mean? It means that jail is probably a lot safer than prison. While you will be sharing your jail cell with virtually everyone arrested that night, most people will just want to get the heck out of there. Unless you go out of your way to show what a tough guy you are—or, in those rare circumstances when someone takes a real dislike to you—you should be pretty safe. Don't make excessive eye contact, and speak as little as possible.

If trouble seems to be a-brewing between the other inmates, stay out of it. If you feel you're a target, tell the guards as soon as possible. In some jails, you are entitled to talk to a supervisor or some administrator whose job it is to keep prisoners happy. Remember, it pays to be polite—even to your jailers. All it takes is one unhappy administrator and your paperwork ends up at the bottom of the pile.

ONE ASSAULT TOO MANY: In one of the most notorious police brutality cases of all time, Haitian immigrant Abner Louima was hauled into a Brooklyn precinct in 1997 and then sexually assaulted in the bathroom— by cops. Officer Justin Volpe ended up pleading guilty to the assault, and Officer Charles Schwarz was found guilty of assisting him, and of obstruction of justice. Two other cops were convicted of obstruction as well. Louima, naturally, filed suit against the NYPD and the City of New York to the tune of millions of dollars. The case sparked national outrage and a heated debate on how much police power was too much—and who was watching out for the ordinary citizen.

Your Time

One of the safe subjects of conversation in jail is jail procedure. Will you get to eat again? What's going to happen next? How long have you been in here? What are the guards like? Keep your eyes and ears open to figure out how things are done. It's quite likely that at least one of your fellow inmates has been here before. See if you can get your questions answered. But remember to steer clear of dangerous topics—such as what you've been arrested for. Or what they've been arrested for. Get it clear in your own mind, but don't discuss.

Street Law Concept #89: Hearing

You've already heard about the arraignment, which is a type of hearing. You might encounter many, many others as your case goes further. A hearing usually involves the presentation of some evidence to decide a legal matter. It almost always takes place in front of a judge or another type of magistrate.

Your Health

Most jails have a doctor on duty around the clock. If you came in with injuries, they should be treated immediately. If you begin to feel sick or have any health concerns, you should tell the guards and demand to see a doctor as soon as possible. If the cops have beaten you up or caused at least some of your injuries, ask the doctor to take photographs when he examines you.

A REAL PRISON BREAK?: "Vincent van Gogh" had intense pain in both his forearms. Unfortunately, he was also in jail in Tampa, so all he got was aspirin. Eight days after his August 1995 arrest, van Gogh was finally allowed to see a doctor at Tampa General. The doctor immediately diagnosed van Gogh with not one but two broken arms. Van Gogh immediately filed a lawsuit against jail officials for refusing him medical treatment.

YOUR DAY IN COURT

In most systems, you're entitled to a hearing within forty-eight hours. If you're waiting longer than that, complain to your lawyer.

A word of warning for all you dreamers out there: your appearance in court is not going to be a happy little revenge fantasy where he scolds the cops for arresting you, apologizes for your time in jail, and sends you on your merry way. This judge is working an assembly-line shift of one suspected crook after another. In most circumstances, he won't even be talking to you.

THEY'RE ONLY HUMAN, TOO: Brooklyn judge "Boss Hogg" was indicted for official misconduct and bribe-taking in August 2003. Hogg apparently accepted cash, gifts, and expensive cigars to fix divorce cases. Though Hogg denied the charges, prosecutors are still planning to try him—after lining up his accomplices, including the court clerk. Meanwhile, Hogg—perhaps in an effort to lessen his possible sentence—has agreed to testify against his nephew "Roscoe P. Coltrane" (also a judge) on charges that Roscoe skimmed $200,000 from a ninety-one-year-old aunt.

Your Lawyer

By now, you're probably itching to talk to someone, anyone. Well, good news: here's your lawyer. Talk away. Everything you say will be between you and her.

If you didn't contact a lawyer yourself, then you're facing a court-appointed attorney, maybe for the first time. This lawyer—either a private attorney or a public defender—is overworked, underpaid, and represents a dozen people like you. This doesn't mean that she's not a good lawyer—it just means that you won't have a lot of time to leisurely talk out your future plans. If you've been smart, you've gone over the incident and have all the facts ready to tell your defense attorney.

Things Your Attorney Might Want to Know

1. Time and place of your arrest
2. What you were doing
3. Whom you were with
4. How the cops approached you
5. If there was any violence, either from cops or participants
6. What the search was like
7. Whether anyone witnessed any part of the whole encounter
8. Any prior convictions or trouble with the law
9. What you do for a living (to show how responsible you are)

If the attorney does not ask "Did you do it?" don't be surprised. An attorney's main job is to argue your side of the case, and to guide you through courtroom procedure. Similarly, don't waste his time by crying and appealing to his sense of justice if you're really guilty. It's more important to be honest with your lawyer and give him the facts that will help him help you.

Your lawyer is the closest thing you have to a friend here. Be polite to the point of being friendly. Do not get bossy. If you have questions about the procedure, ask him. Your lawyer will also be speaking for you in court. Give him all the information he asks for, and make it clear that you just want to go home.

The Hearing

Various jurisdictions have different procedures after the arrest. Some have a probable-cause hearing, where a judge evaluates whether the cops had enough probable cause to arrest you. Some go straight to the arraignment, which is usually the first time that you make an appearance before the court, and where lawyers will negotiate your state-set bail.

> **FIGHTING THE PLEDGE:** Little "Goldilocks" was living with her mother, "Mama Bear," when "Papa Bear" heard that the school wanted Goldilocks to recite the Pledge of Allegiance. Being an atheist—as well as a doctor and a lawyer—Papa Bear brought a lawsuit saying that this was unconstitutional. The Ninth Circuit Court agreed, stating that the "under God" part of the Pledge of Allegiance violated the First Amendment. Unfortunately, Mama Bear didn't see the problem with the Pledge and neither, says Mama Bear, did Goldilocks. Papa Bear was set to argue in the Supreme Court and wanted Goldilocks to watch, but the court

felt it would be inappropriate. Why? Because one of
the key questions in the case was whether Papa Bear
had standing to file the suit on Goldilocks' behalf.
Since Papa Bear and Mama Bear had divorced, Papa
Bear had only partial custody. The court felt that it
wasn't right for Goldilocks to watch custody argu-
ments between her parents. (Fun fact: Mama Bear's
lawyer was Kenneth Starr, the guy who tried to prosecute President Clinton.)

The DA you're facing is doing the pretrial-hearing
shift. She has your file, including a list of all your prior
arrests and the police report of this arrest. She represents
the cops' version of your arrest. She's not out to get you—
she probably can't keep your name straight from the rest
of the troublemakers they brought in today. In fact, don't
be surprised if the DA and your lawyer went to school
together. It's been known to happen.

You won't be doing much talking during the arraignment. Mostly, you and your lawyer will have decided what
your plea will be, and what the possible penalties will be.
The lawyer will state your plea to the judge, and the judge
will decide bail. The DA might argue the case one way
or another, but in all likelihood, this hearing will be short
and to the point.

TAKING THE HIGH ROAD: After being accused of dealing
drugs, "Isaac Newton" of Norristown, Pennsylvania,
was finally hauled before the court. His attorney
appealed to the judge to lower the bail from the current
$150,000, arguing that his client was a law-abiding
citizen who wouldn't dream of fleeing. Just as his

attorney was winding down, Newton sprinted out of the courtroom and onto the streets. Cops caught him about an hour later. Needless to say, his bail was increased to $500,000, which kept the fleet-footed, slow-witted Newton solidly in custody.

Your Plea

Traditionally, there are three different pleas:

Guilty	"Okay, I admit it—I did what the cops are accusing me of. Just go easy on me, okay?"
Not Guilty	"I am not guilty of what the police are accusing me of. Kindly keep your insinuations to yourself."
Nolo Contendere	"I am not going to contest the police's version of events, but I'm not admitting to anything either. I just want this horrible ordeal to go away."

A not-guilty plea is not the same thing as saying "I'm innocent." A lawyer can represent you as not being guilty for a variety of reasons—self-defense, insanity, etc. Remember that *guilty* and *not guilty* are legal terms. A lawyer cannot ethically argue that you are innocent of a crime if he has direct knowledge of your guilt. He can however argue that you're "not guilty," which means that he's arguing with the cops' version of the facts. This is a gray area of professional ethics that confuses and traps many attorneys.

How you plead is up to you and your lawyer. In many minor cases, your lawyer will advise you to "take a plea," or plea-bargain.

Street Law Concept #90: Plea-Bargain

In this process, the accused (you) and the prosecution negotiate a mutually satisfactory arrangement. Usually this means that you will plead to a lesser charge to get a reduced sentence.

Whether you take the plea or not is entirely your call. Do not ever plead guilty to anything that you didn't do. However, if you are planning to fight this all the way to the Supreme Court, just remember this: courts, trials, lawyers, etc., take up a lot of money and a lot of time. Fighting long legal battles is the hobby of the extremely bored or extremely rich. Just take that into consideration before standing by your guns and planning to blaze your way to glory.

DIVAS DON'T DO TRIAL: When legendary singer Diana Ross was arrested for drunk driving in Tucson, Arizona, she wasn't planning on doing any jail time like us ordinary folks—despite her conviction. In February of 2003, Ross entered a no-contest plea to driving under the influence and was sentenced to forty-eight hours in jail. She was also sentenced to a year of probation. If she had gone to trial and been found guilty, Ross was looking at a minimum of ten days in jail, plus a fine. The plea bargain was hard-won for Ross, who asserted that she felt "coerced" into taking a Breathalyzer test by the cops' "threatening tone." The judge didn't buy that, but did approve the plea bargain.

All this has one caveat: never, ever, plead guilty for something that you didn't do.

Changing Lawyers

If you feel that your attorney just can't cut it, you are entitled to complain to either an investigator in the public defender's office or to the judge herself. This is rarely advised unless your attorney (1) is really incompetent, (2) refuses to see you or answer your calls, or (3) pressures you into pleading guilty. If this is the case, your best bet is to state that you and the lawyer differ so much that you simply cannot work together to present a defense. It's a tough road to switch public defenders this way, but you are legally entitled to a competent defense.

You can switch to a private lawyer whenever you want, but too many attorney changes can hurt your case. Whether a private attorney is better than a public defender is a matter of personal opinion, and dependent on the particulars of your case.

Malicious Prosecution

Like malicious or false arrest, malicious prosecution is not easy to prove. But it does happen.

Street Law Concept #91: Malicious Prosecution
This occurs when the prosecution came after you (a) without probable cause and (b) with malice.

Street Law Concept #92: Malice
In this instance, it means that the prosecution knowingly acted with the actual intent of falsely prosecuting you. In some states, it can also mean that the prosecution willfully disregarded the possibility that you might be maliciously prosecuted.

A case for malicious prosecution occurs after your trial—it's actually a civil suit. You'll have to show that the malicious prosecution caused you physical injury or injured your property or your reputation. All arrests, including legitimate ones, cause *some* damage to the reputation or to the person—so you'll have to work hard to prove your injuries.

The Sentence

For the purposes of this book, most of your sentence should be time served, probation, a small fine, or jail time. That's usually what happens with run-of-the-mill, nonviolent misdemeanors. If you have priors or went down for something else, you might be looking at something more serious.

Street Law Concept #93: Probation

Probation has many different names in many different jurisdictions. Basically, it means that you are released without imprisonment, but you are subject to certain conditions. You may be supposed to stay away from drugs or certain people or simply stay out of legal trouble (no arrests). Your probation will last a certain length of time. If you violate the terms of your probation, you will be yanked back into the justice system, usually to face your old charge as well as your new one.

A MOUTHFUL: When cops arrived at his doorstep to arrest him for beating his wife, "Spartacus" expressed his opinion of cops the old-fashioned way—by spitting in a cop's face. Bad idea. Under an Oklahoma law that makes it a felony to "place bodily fluids" on law enforcement officers (for fear of AIDS, etc.), Spartacus was sentenced to life. You read that right—life. Of course, the judge took Spartacus's priors into account, and since Spartacus already had a couple of felony convictions—including ones for rape and burglary—the sentence might make a little more sense.

What you should be aiming for is a dismissal of all the charges. This might be wishful thinking, but the DA doesn't always decide to pursue every case in front of him. The second best thing is probation, or an adjournment on contemplation of a dismissal (the name varies from state to state). This means you will be placed on probation for a time (usually one year). If you're good during that year, the court will dismiss the charges. In many cases, your record will be cleared of the arrest as well. If you're not, then you'll get rearrested for this charge, and for whatever naughtiness you were doing to violate probation.

One More Time: Be Nice to the Clerk!: "Shylock" was serving a seven-year sentence for child molestation in Atlanta, Georgia. Unfortunately, the Fulton County clerk's office didn't give prison officials his correct release date. As a result, Shylock spent two extra years in prison, getting released in 2003 rather than in 2001 as scheduled. Proving he's a true American, Shylock is suing head clerk "Portia" for $2.5 million. True, for child molestation some people just want to throw away the key, but that pesky Constitution has a thing or two to say about that . . .

If probation isn't in your future, you'll need to think about some other details. If there's a fine, the court offi-